Laboratory Investigations

for

AP* Environmental Science

William Molnar

PEOPLES
PUBLISHING GROUP
299 Market Street, Saddle Brook, NJ 07663

Publisher: Tom Maksym

Executive Editor: Steven Jay Griffel

Vice President, Production and Manufacturing: Doreen Smith

Creative Director/Assistant Vice President: Amy Rosen

Project Manager: Steven Genzano

Production Editor: Carol Deckert

Designer: Carol Deckert

Proofreader: Michael O'Neill

Illustrators/Technical Art: Carol Deckert, Sal Esposito, Steven Genzano, Yadiro Henriquez, Alexis Rodriguez

Cartographer: Sharon MacGregor

Cover Design: Amy Rosen, Michele Sakow, Cristina Castro Pelka

Permissions Manager: Kristine Liebman

Photo Research: Pat Smith, Robert E. Lee

Image Credits: Cover images, center, Lightscapes Photography, Inc./Corbis, top 2 images, © Royalty Free/Corbis, bottom 2 images, Photos.com; title page, Photos.com; pp. iii-v, Photos.com; p. 1, 2, Photos.com; p. 4, Photo courtesy of J.D. Wilson, Department of Earth and Atmospheric Sciences, University of Alberta, Canada; p. 12, University of Nevada, Las Vegas; p. 14, WVU Extension Service; p. 16, Green/Getty Images; p. 19, Photodisc Green/Getty Images; p. 24, Green/Getty Images; p. 25, (top) Photos.com, (bottom) courtesy of William Molnar; p. 27, Michael Going/Getty Images; p. 33, U.S. Geological Survey, September 30, 2003, A Tapestry of Time and Terrain, in National Atlas of the United States, http://nationalatlas.gov; p. 35, Macduff/Getty; p. 41, Photos.com; p. 47, (top) Photos.com, (bottom) Courtesy of the United States Interior Department; p. 50, Photos.com; p. 51, (top) Photos.com, (bottom) Green/Getty Images; p. 56, Green/Getty Images; p. 59, Photos.com; p. 60, Photos.com; p. 63, (top) Photodisc/Getty Images, (bottom) Photos.com; p. 67, © E.R. Degginger/Earthscenes; p. 77, Alan Kearney/Getty Images; p. 79, © John Gerlach/Earthscenes; p. 85, Photos.com; p. 99, 101, 109, Photos.com; p. 115, © Austin J. Stevens/Animals Animals; p. 119, Photos.com; p. 127, Frank Blackburn/Getty Images; p. 133, Jon Riley/Getty Images; p. 145, Paul Harris/Getty Images; p. 149, Photos.com; p. 163, Photos.com; p. 167, Photos.com; p. 171 (top), Photodisc/Getty, (bottom), Photos.com; p. 175 (top), Photos.com, (bottom), John Thornton; p. 179, Photos.com; p. 183, © Stephen Dalton/OSF/Earthscenes; p. 189, Photos.com; p. 193 (top), Photos.com, (bottom), courtesy of William Molnar; p. 197, Photos.com; p. 201 (top), Peter Parks/AFP/Getty Images, (bottom), Photos.com; p. 209, Photos.com; back cover images, top 2 images, © Royalty Free/Corbis, bottom 2 images, Photos.com

* AP is a registered trademark of the College Board, which was not involved in the production of, and does not endorse, this book.

ISBN 1-4138-0487-X

Table *of* Contents

LABORATORY INVESTIGATIONS

Laboratory Investigations for AP Environmental Science

Preface

You are about to embark on an exciting journey. AP Environmental Science is a unique course because it is an applied science that focuses on problem solving. There is very little pure theory. You have already learned some basic principles of biology, chemistry, physics and mathematics. *Lab Investigations in AP Environmental Science* will help you apply that knowledge by examining the natural environment and considering how human activity is changing it. In addition, you will search for viable resolutions to environmental problems. Along the way you will also learn some political science, sociology, and economics.

You should treat the word *science* as a verb—an action word. You will learn much more by being actively involved than just by reading. Environmental Science holds many opportunities to learn by doing. This is a program tailor-made for curious students who enjoy taking an active role in their education.

USING THE BOOK

The main approach of this book is to examine how the biosphere works and changes naturally and then investigate how humans are affecting it. A major emphasis will be on sustainability of ecosystems and resources and on human responsibility.

Investigation 1 is a series of twelve field studies and long-term projects. One or more of these can be done at any time of the school year, time permitting, and in any order. Most are designed to require a minimum amount of equipment, and many can be done indoors with little problem.

The rationale for the order of the remaining investigations is that to understand human effect on the environment, one must appreciate how the Earth works as if humans were not here. The early labs deal with physical earth systems, plate tectonics, heat absorption and climate, protected natural areas, and the tides. The next few relate to resources, soils and water. Biological systems are studied next, with labs on productivity, food chains and trophic levels, predation, and biodiversity.

Once there is a comprehension of how the natural world works, you will probe various aspects of human population growth and their effects on the Earth. After looking at the impact of the size of human populations, you will turn to investigate how humans meet their energy needs and the effects of those methods.

Lastly you will look into the effects that over six billion people in a growing industrial society have on the biosphere. Many of our environmental predicaments are due to rapid human population growth and unsustainable allocation and use of resources. For example, transportation systems, water use, growth of cities and suburbs, agriculture, energy production and consumption, and waste production and disposal all are carried out in unsustainable ways.

AP Environmental Science is a college-level course, and the experiments and projects should be conducted at that level. Consequently, the format for writing up your results must, in many cases, be more sophisticated than the ways to which you may be accustomed. All your lab experiments and reports should contain the following parts:

Abstract

This is a synopsis of the investigation. It should be written in concise English and be not more than 200 words. Assume that the reader has some background knowledge in the area of your investigation. The beginning sentences should indicate the subject of the investigation and what your goals are. The middle part of the abstract should tell about your observations and measurements and what you concluded. You could include pertinent data that stands out as a result of the experiment.

Introduction

Here you will state the objectives of the investigation, why you are performing this experiment, and why it is important. In many cases it is also where you predict your results. It is important to state your objectives clearly, because they will again be addressed in your conclusions at the end of the experiment. At that point your objectives will have to be analyzed to find out whether you were successful.

Materials

This is simply a list of equipment, chemicals, and instruments you used to complete this study. It should be comprehensive enough to let someone else easily gather materials to repeat your procedures.

Procedure

The objective here is to give others enough directions to perform your experiment themselves. Normally procedures are written in the first person, because they tell what you did. You can organize them as a list, but be sure of the order of steps. Do not outline too much, but include sufficient detail to allow the experiment to be repeated.

Data Tables

The data table is a graphical organizer to record the data you gather in the investigation. It is important to read through the whole experiment to determine what information needs to be documented. A good table of data will make doing the calculations more organized. Keep in mind what data will be used in the actual calculations and graphs; structure the table so that the initial measurements come before the needed values.

Calculations

In doing this part be sure to organize your work. Show numbers and calculations in order on the paper. Show the equation used, then how you substituted the values into it, and finally the result. Always use proper units. If the units cancel out correctly, then you can be confident you set the problem up properly. Underline your final answers.

Graphs

Not all investigations will have graphs, but when they do be sure to use proper form. The independent variable is always on the *x*-axis (horizontal) and the dependent variable is plotted on the *y*-axis (vertical). When setting up the scales, mark off the axes in proportional units, even if the data are not uniformly spaced. Label each axis and give the units of measure. Plot the points as accurately as you can and connect the points with a smooth continuous line of best fit. If more than one line is to be plotted, label each one. Do not use a legend on the side. Give the graph a title.

Results

This is the heart of the investigation. It is here that you discuss and analyze the results. Outline whether your data were as you expected and whether there were any sources of error. Based on your outcomes, suggest ways to improve the investigation.

Conclusion

You can use the questions at the end of the investigations for guidance. The conclusion is where you give overall perspective to your experiment. You should summarize your findings and discuss any implications that lead from them. In the conclusion you may opt to discuss extensions to the lab and suggestions for further areas of study.

AP Environmental Science is a stimulating and vibrant course. As you will see, there are no simplistic answers to environmental problems. You are about to set out on a year of exploration that will make you more aware of your natural and human-made surroundings. It will also improve your skills as a critical thinker and help you look at all sides of a problem to search for the best solution. But don't sit back and be passive. Be an active learner and participate—get involved! And enjoy the year.

William Molnar

Field Studies
and Extended Projects

Project

INTRODUCTION

One of the major goals of this course is to let you conduct field studies or experiments that demand much more extended periods of observation than you have previously experienced. Investigation 1 is designed to give you rich ideas for choosing such an extended project and some simple guidelines to get started.

In most of your previous science classes the labs have been one or two class periods in duration, and you followed a detailed set of directions. In this course you will have the opportunity—and the challenge—of designing your own experiment or long-term study. Through these explorations you will better learn to:

➤ Observe environmental systems in detail

➤ Design and execute well-planned experiments

➤ Design and implement well thought out tables of data for organizing and collecting information

➤ Use proper techniques and equipment

➤ Draw conclusions based on your observed data and calculations

➤ Write a clear and concise report of your findings and why they support your conclusions

➤ Propose ways to extend your results by means of further study

Read carefully through all 12 suggested projects before choosing. Several are actual extended outdoor activities where you will collect data in the field and draw conclusions. Others will require you to analyze a system to look for patterns and some require you to keep a journal of observations over an extended period of time.

These inquiries can be tried in any order at any time of the academic year. However, it is recommended that local climate conditions dictate when some of the outdoor exercises are attempted. Most of the projects can be carried out indoors with a minimum of special equipment.

1-1 Stream Water Quality and Macroinvertebrate Population Comparison

PURPOSE

➤ Measure water quality conditions in a local stream or river

➤ Collect macroinvertebrates and correlate the fauna to stream conditions

Materials

- test kits (or CBLs) and other tools to measure:
  - water depth
  - rate of flow
  - turbidity
  - dissolved oxygen
  - pH
  - nitrates
  - water temperature
- kick net
- camera and/or drawing materials

Fig. 1-1

The abundance and kinds of macroinvertebrates populating a body of fresh water are good indicators of its overall water quality.

Procedure

Step 1 Using test kits or CBLs, measure the water depth, rate of flow, turbidity, temperature, pH, dissolved oxygen and nitrates in a stream on a regular basis. It is recommended to do so once a month through the spring. (*Note:* See Investigation 12 for a review of materials and procedures for these and related water quality tests.)

Step 2   After reading through this procedure completely, design a data table to record your observations and all test results over the study period.

Step 3   Record the conditions of the stream. Use methods such as:

- Drawing a map or taking a picture of your testing site.
- Describing what the banks are like. Are they stable? eroding? undercut? Does the water reach the base of both banks? Is the water variable over time?
- Describing the vegetation. Are the banks covered with vegetation? Does the vegetation cover the stream?
- Recording the surroundings. Are the banks wide or close to roads, buildings, parking lots, clear cuts, etc?
- Examining the stream bottom. Is it muddy, rocky, or covered in sediments?
- Analyzing any engineering. Are there bridge abutments, rip-rap, culverts, etc?
- Observing what the channel is like. Is it straight? If curved, how much so?

Step 4   Use a kick net to collect macroinvertebrates at your test site.

Step 5   Record the types of macroinvertebrates you collected and their numbers.

(Macroinvertebrates are good indicators of stream water quality. For example, stone flies, caddis flies and hellgrammites indicate good water quality; crawfish and sowbugs can be found in water of fair quality; and leeches and some snails are indications of poor water quality.)

Step 6   Graph your measured water quality data. Try to correlate these data to the macroinvertebrates you collected. Does your water testing bear out these indicators? Why or why not?

1-2 Comparison of Daily Weather Data with Microclimate Data

PURPOSE

➤ Collect weather data at the microclimate level and compare and contrast to the weather conditions reported locally

Materials

- instruments to measure:
  - air temperature
  - wind speed and direction
  - relative humidity
- Internet access

Procedure

Step 1 Go to a Web site that gives the local weather for your school area. One possibility:
http://www.weather.com

Step 2 Using your own weather instruments, measure the temperature, the wind speed and direction, and the relative humidity at several locations around your school grounds. At each site, measurements should be taken at ground level and at 50 cm and 1 m above ground level.

Fig. 1-2: Ground Level Weather Monitors

Step 3 After reading through this procedure completely, design a data table to record your information.

Step 4 Describe each location where you recorded your measurements. Include observations such as:

   a. Is this spot in the open? Are there buildings, trees, or land forms that would influence your measurements?

   b. What is the ground cover like—vegetation, soil, concrete, blacktop, brick, or other?

   c. Are there any organisms that live in the immediate test area? Do they vary from site to site?

Step 5 Analyze your results.

   a. Do the data implicate micro-climate involvement?

   b. Do the measurements in different locations vary? If so, how and why?

   c. If the area of your measurements is covered with vegetation, does it vary with location? How could the vegetation be related to the local conditions?

Hurricane Tracking and Prediction

PURPOSE

➤ Track and project the paths of hurricanes, using regional weather data and other factors to make predictions

➤ Research and analyze long-term tropical storm patterns and their impact on human communities

Materials

• Internet access

Fig. 1-3

A hurricane-tracking map for the East and Gulf Coasts over the 2001 season. Latitude and longitude scales are included for reference.

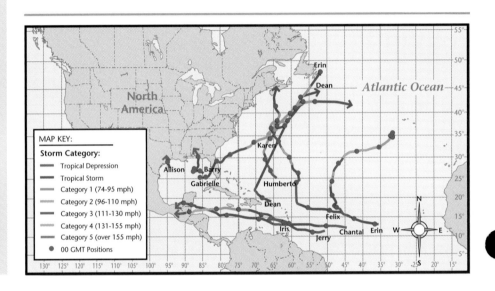

Procedure

Step 1 During the hurricane season, track the paths of hurricanes along the East Coast or, in the eastern Pacific Ocean, of tropical cyclones. Downloadable maps, which can be used to plot the storms as they occur, are found at:
http://www.usatoday.com/weather/wtrack.htm

Step 2 Various Web sites will let you monitor tracking data along with the regional weather conditions that might influence the path of the storm. The National Oceanographic and Atmospheric Administration (NOAA) is a good site at:
http://www.nhc.noaa.gov/index.shtml
This site also has tracking charts at the bottom of the page.

Step 3 Predict and map landfall for each of the hurricanes you track. What weather conditions and other factors lead you to your predictions? Justify your forecast.

Step 4 Research the following questions:

    a. How do hurricanes form? Why are they usually late summer and autumn events?

    b. How does El Niño affect the hurricane season?

    c. Collect data on hurricane damage on the East Coast since 1900. Describe the trend in the human death toll over that time. Why has it changed in that way?

    d. Collect data on property damage costs over the same time period. Why is that the trend? What has happened since 1900 to influence these results?

Testing for Tropospheric Ozone Pollution

PURPOSE

➣ Prepare and carry out tests for tropospheric ozone pollution

➣ Analyze the ozone pollution test results for local variation and possible impact on human health

Materials

- beaker calibrated in milliliters
- corn starch
- hot plate and magnetic stirrer
- potassium iodide
- filter paper

Optional:
- sling psychrometer or CBL

Procedure

Step 1   Place 100 mL of water in a beaker, then add 5 g of corn starch.

Step 2   On a hot plate with a magnetic stirrer, heat the mixture until it gels and becomes somewhat translucent.

Step 3   Remove the mixture from the heat. Add 1.0 g of potassium iodide and stir well, then let the mixture cool to a paste.

Step 4   Lay a piece of filter paper (or coffee filter) on your lab table and brush the paste on it, being sure to cover it completely and uniformly.

Step 5   Turn the paper over and repeat Step 4. The paper can now be used for testing, but it is better to allow the paper to dry in the dark. Keep away from direct sunlight. (*Lab Hint*: Fast drying can be accomplished in a microwave at low power for 30–60 seconds.)

Step 6   Cut the filter paper in 1-inch strips and store in an airtight container such as a zip-lock bag in the dark. Potassium iodide is sensitive to moisture and light. CAUTION: Wash your hands thoroughly when done. Potassium iodide, although not toxic, is a mild basic salt and can cause a skin irritation.

Step 7   Select sites near your school and/or home. The test strips should be able to hang freely, but not in direct sunlight. Try sites like your classroom, rest rooms, gym, cafeteria, teacher copying room, parking lots, etc.

Step 8   To test for ozone, moisten a test strip in distilled water and hang it at a collection site out of direct sunlight for eight hours. Then seal it in an airtight container until you are ready to measure your results.

Step 9   When you are ready to record your results, dip the paper in distilled water and observe the color. Use the color in the area of the most pronounced change. To determine the ozone concentration, you will need to determine the Schoenbein Number. For this use the following Web site:

http://teachertech.rice.edu/Participants/lee/colorscale.html

Step 10 The relative humidity affects your results because potassium iodide is moisture sensitive. High humidity gives a high Schoenbein Number. To correct for the humidity you must first determine the local relative humidity. Use a sling psychrometer or CBL or, if the humidity cannot be determined by experiment, the local weather report. Round this figure to the nearest 10%.

Step 11 Now, with you local relative humidity, go to the chart at the following Web site:

http://teachertech.rice.edu/Participants/lee/Images/graph2.jpg

Find your humidity on the *x*-axis and draw a line up to the line for the local humidity. Then draw a line horizontally to the *y*-axis to read the corrected ozone concentration in parts per billion.

Step 12 Analyze your data.

a. Did the readings change from site to site?

b. What was going on in the areas with the highest ozone readings? Was there electronic equipment or machinery? Take into account other strong oxidizers, such as oxides of nitrogen, that may influence your results.

c. Make some judgments about ozone levels in the areas you tested. Why did you get the results you recorded?

d. What are the health hazards of elevated ozone levels? What can be done to alleviate them?

e. How is tropospheric ozone different from stratospheric ozone?

1-5 Global Warming and Atmospheric CO₂ Correlation

PURPOSE

➤ Research carbon dioxide concentrations in the atmosphere for the last 420,000 years

➤ Correlate the data mathematically to global temperatures

Materials

• Internet access

Fig. 1-4

These data reveal how short-term fluxes in atmospheric carbon dioxide closely track long-term trends.

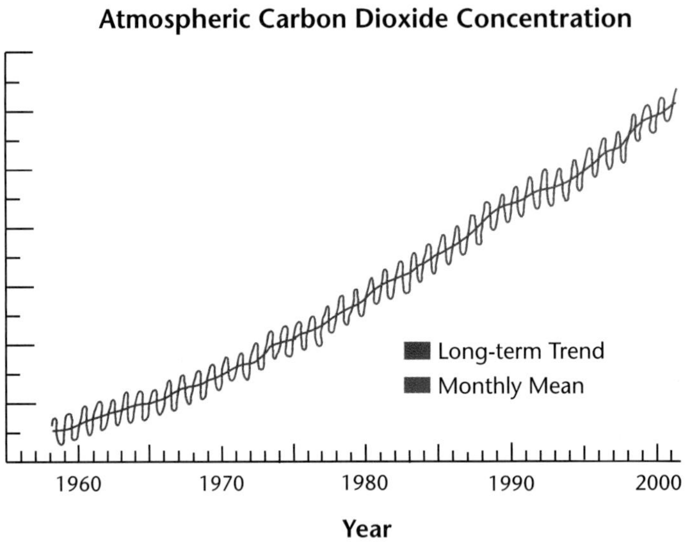

Atmospheric Carbon Dioxide Concentration

Legend: Long-term Trend, Monthly Mean

x-axis: 1960, 1970, 1980, 1990, 2000 — Year

Procedure

Step 1   You will need to select intervals for data point entries over the last 420,000 years.

Step 2   Go to the following Web site and enter the years and CO₂ concentrations in a spreadsheet:
ftp://ftp.ncdc.noaa.gov/pub/data/paleo/icecore/antarctica/vostok/co2nat.txt

Step 3   Go to the following Web site and enter the years and temperatures in a spreadsheet:
ftp://ftp.ngdc.noaa.gov/paleo/icecore/antarctica/vostok/deutnat.txt
The age of the core sample is in column 2 and the temperature is in column 4.

Step 4   From the spreadsheets, make a graph. Plot time along the x-axis. Make two y-axes, one on either side of the x-axis. On the left y-axis, plot the carbon dioxide data, and on the right y-axis, plot the temperature records.

Step 5 Analyze your data.

    a. Describe how carbon dioxide concentrations and temperatures vary over time.

    b. Tell how the graphs change compared to each other. Is there evidence of a cause-and-effect relationship between CO_2 and temperature? Explain.

    c. What could cause the carbon dioxide levels to change over the time studied? How could orbital changes, plate tectonics, and/or ocean currents play a role?

    d. Describe patterns for any Ice Ages that occurred during the period of the study.

    e. Where are we today in relation to the graphed data? What lies in the near future? What in the data makes you believe in that change?

Step 6 Soils may absorb enormous amounts of carbon dioxide. Describe how changes in land usage over the last 50 to 100 years have had an effect on this sequestering ability.

Step 7 How are insurance companies and the Pentagon reacting to the impact of global warming?

Step 8 Outline five environmental effects of global warming.

1-6 Elevated CO$_2$ Levels and Plant Growth

PURPOSE

➤ Conduct an experiment on effects of CO$_2$ enrichment on plant growth

➤ Compare your experimental results with available data from related experiments on enhanced crop growth

Materials

- 3 kinds of naturally growing plants (or crops like peas, beans, radishes, etc.)
- 6 growing chambers (such as small aquariums)
- potting soil (1 large bag)
- plastic tubing
- 3M hydrochloric acid
- calcium carbonate
- Internet access and/or print materials for research

Procedure

Step 1 Select 3 different plants that grow in your region for testing.

Step 2 You will grow the plants in growth chambers of the same size and composition. For each plant tested, you will need two containers, one for the experiment and one as a control.

Step 3 Set up growth chambers so that all have the same amount of soil. Prepare the soil in a large pail or basin so that the composition is uniform for all 6 chambers.

Step 4 The containers must be able to be loosely sealed from the room atmosphere. The only variable must be the level of carbon dioxide, so place the chambers where the temperature and sunlight are the same.

Step 5 Carbon dioxide can be produced by reacting calcium carbonate with 3M hydrochloric acid and transferring to the three experimental chambers by tubing. The volume of carbon dioxide can be calculated stoichiometrically from the amount of calcium carbonate used. The concentration of the gas can be calculated by measuring the volume of the chambers and converting the units to liters.

(*Note*: An alternate method, for direct measurement of the carbon dioxide concentration, is Vernier's Carbon Dioxide Gas Sensor. This device connects with a CBL and graphing calculator, or a Palm Pilot, or directly to your computer with Logger Pro® software.)

Step 6 Plant the seeds in the soils so that they are evenly spaced. Water the soil and add the carbon dioxide. Set up a timetable that you will follow for adding the gas over the duration of the experiment.

Step 7 Set up a journal where you can write up your procedure, show your calculations and record your observations over the course of the investigation. Measure:

- germination time
- growth rate
- leaf area
- stem branching
- amount of vegetation or produce
- other pertinent observations regarding the effect of the excess carbon dioxide.

Step 8 Analyze your findings. Compare the growth of the experimental groups to that of the controls.

Step 9 Research other experiments that seek to find the effects of elevated carbon dioxide levels on plants. What were their results? The Duke University Free Air Carbon Enrichment (FACE) study has some interesting initial findings.

Step 10 Currently, the concentration of CO_2 in the atmosphere is a little over 370 parts per million by volume (ppmv). The average rate of increase has been 1.4 ppmv per year since 1972. This would give an atmospheric concentration of over 500 ppmv in one hundred years, if the rate of absorption also stays the same.

   a. Comment on the often stated claim that increased carbon dioxide levels would increase plant growth and, therefore, remove the gas from the atmosphere due to increased photosynthesis.

   b. Describe some research on how crops react to the increase of the gas. What other factors, such as nutrition levels, fertilizer requirements, pests, etc., are involved?

Step 11 Describe ways in which you would change the experiment you conducted. What other results would you expect?

1-7 Natural vs. Synthetic Chemical Fertilizers

PURPOSE

➤ Compare crop samples grown from natural fertilizers with those from synthetic chemical fertilizers

Fig. 1-6

Commercial fertilizers use a numbering system to indicate the proportions of key chemical components. These products also give rates of application for various crops and soils.

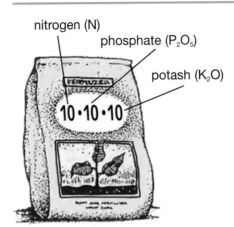

nitrogen (N)

phosphate (P$_2$O$_5$)

potash (K$_2$O)

10·10·10

Materials

- 2 small garden plots
- soil test kit
- Berlese funnel
- basic garden tools
- compost (or manure) for at least 1 meter square
- chemical fertilizer for at least 1 meter square
- crop seeds (such as peas, beans, or radish)

Procedure

Step 1 Set up two garden plots of the same size, from 1 to several meters square. They must be in an adjoining area where soil, sunlight, and terrain are uniform and should not have been artificially planted or fertilized previously. Remove any existing vegetation.

Step 2 After reading through all steps of this procedure, plan a journal where you will outline your procedure, label and map your plots, and record your data in tables.

Step 3 With a soil test kit, determine the pH and the nitrate, phosphate, and potassium levels of both plots by taking several samples from different parts of each plot. Mix the samples together before testing. Also determine the soil texture of each sample. Use a Berlese funnel to identify any soil organisms you find in each sample. Record all these data in your journal.

Step 4 In one plot add 15–20 cm of compost and/or manure to the top of the bare soil. Then, using a pitchfork or shovel, thoroughly mix it into the upper 30 cm of soil.

Step 5 On the other plot, prepare the ground by thoroughly turning over the upper 30 cm of soil with a pitchfork or shovel. Be sure to break up the big clods. Add chemical fertilizer from a garden or farm supply store at the recommended rate for your crop.

Step 6 Plant your crops at the spacing and depth recommended on the seed package. Be sure to water your crops if there is insufficient rainfall.

Step 7 Every four to five days during the growing season, measure and record the pH and the nitrate, phosphate, and potassium levels of the two plots. Using a Berlese funnel, collect, identify, and record soil organisms at the same time.

Step 8 Measure and record the growth of the crop plants in both plots.

Step 9 If it is possible, collect runoff water after a heavy rain and measure the pH and the nitrate, phosphate, and potassium levels in the runoff.

Step 10 When your plants produce a crop, measure the amount of produce from each plot. (You may opt to do a comparative taste test as well.)

Step 11 After you harvest your crop, test the soil chemistry and soil organisms one last time.

Step 12 In your journal, describe how the test measurements changed in each plot over time and if there was a corresponding change in the plants.

Step 13 Analyze your experimental results. What conclusions can you draw as a result of this experiment?

1-8 Effect of Soil Humus on Composting Rates

PURPOSE

➤ Compare decomposition rates of various compost materials in soils of different humus content

Fig. 1-7

A home gardener's compost pile. In soil rich with humus, millions of organisms feed on and break down organic material, both plant and animal, releasing nutrients into the soil. Soils poor in humus do not have the same ability to decompose organic matter.

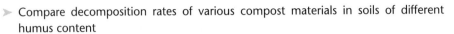

Materials

- 5 or more soil test sites
- 1 soil test kit
- materials to compost, including:
  - white paper strips
  - animal food waste
  - newspaper strips
  - bones
  - aluminum foil
  - egg shells
  - vegetable waste
  - coffee grounds
  - leaves
  - grass clippings

Procedure

Step 1   Select at least five sites with varying amounts of humus, from very rich soils to very poor ones.

Step 2   After reading all steps of this procedure, set up a journal to describe your sites and procedures and to record your data.

Step 3   Using test kits, measure the pH and the nitrate, phosphate, and potassium concentrations at each site.

Step 4   At each site bury samples of each material listed above. Dig a hole about 10 cm deep for each item and then replace the soil on top.

Step 5 Draw a site map for each location so that you can easily relocate each item for observation.

Step 6 Once a week, gently remove the soil from the top of each test item to monitor it for signs of decomposition. Carefully record your observations, and then replace the soil.

Step 7 Note the rate at which each substance decays at each location. List substances from the most decay to the least decay.

Step 8 Analyze your data.

a. Does the same material appear in each list of decay rates in the same position? What did you expect, and which items surprised you by their rates?

b. At the end of your study, compare the overall decay rates of all materials to the amount of humus in the soil.

c. Which materials either did not decay or completely decayed away? How did soil chemistry affect the experiment?

d. How did food items with preservatives decay compared to those without preservatives?

Step 9 Make some comparisons to materials we place in landfills. How long do you think some of those substances take to decay? How can the process be speeded up?

Step 10 Extension Repeat this experiment using red worms (*Eisenia foetida*) to compost your test materials. These worms eat up to their own weight each day, and their castings are an excellent soil conditioner. The worms are inexpensive and easy to keep. You can perform this experiment in a 60 cm × 60 cm × 30 cm aquarium.

1-9 Land Use Changes in Your Area

PURPOSE

➤ Research and record land use changes in your state or a nearby urbanized area

➤ Analyze land use trends for their environmental impact

Materials

- maps of local towns and cities
- access to research library and/or local historical societies
- acetate sheets

Optional:
- GIS (Geographic Information System) mapping program

Procedure

Step 1 Select a region in your state, preferably near an urban center or large metropolitan area. Keep in mind that many cities were first built on flat land, near a coast, or along rivers, which were important for transportation, irrigation, and domestic uses. As the population grew, the town or city spread out into the surrounding countryside.

Step 2 In a notebook, make a table to document current population, total surface area, general topography, flood plains, land use, roads, and infrastructure such as parks, reservoirs, power lines, etc. (This would be a good project for using GIS if you have access to the program.)

Step 3 Research, as far back as you can, maps of the region when it was first settled. You can usually find such information in your local town hall, library, or county assessor's office. From these and other historical resources, record facts such as:

a. How many people lived there?

b. What was the surface area of the town?

c. About what percent of the land was forest, farms, wetland, waterfront buildings, stores and shops, and homes?

d. Where were the roads? What were they constructed of? Where did the materials come from? Where did the roads go?

Step 4 On a large sheet of paper, draw the oldest map you could find. Then, on sheets of clear acetate, draw more recent maps, up to the present, that can overlay the original map. In your notes, document how the land use changed over time.

Step 5   Make a general analysis of your data.

    a. What happened to the best farmland? What is in its place today?

    b. What percent of the land is covered with structures and pavement today, compared to the first map?

    c. Describe at least five significant environmental impacts related to this development.

Step 6   An interesting map to look at is the United States at night. This is a composite of many satellite pictures of the United States. The eastern United States is awash with light and the western states are not as developed, but still not as dark as might be expected.

- Describe how the coast of California from San Francisco to San Diego compares to the surrounding region. Do the same for the east coast from Boston to Richmond.

- Describe the arrangement of lights in the midwestern United States and compare them to the east-coast pattern of lights. Why do you think those patterns exist?

- In the west, why are the lights strung out in lines? What causes that arrangement?

- Comment, based on the map, on how transportation systems affect urban and suburban development.

Fig. 1-8: Satellite Photo of the United States at Night

Step 7   Explain how modern technology can help planners prevent some of the problems of urban sprawl.

1-10 **Toxic Sites in Your Neighborhood**

PURPOSE

➤ Research and analyze environmental problems locally, determining their causes, ecological and public health impacts, and possible resolutions

Materials

- Internet access

Procedure

Step 1 For this extended study, access the following Web site:

http://scorecard.org/

It is an extensive compilation of environmental problems for every state.

Step 2 On the home page of this site, under the U.S. map, there are listed nine environmental issues to be explored by community, state, or region. Select five issues and relate them to a local area of your choosing. (Another option is to enter your zip code in the area called Find Your Community and then track the various problems outlined from that perspective to answer the questions that follow.)

Step 3 Try to link the five issues, searching for common threads:

a. What industries are involved in the problem?

b. Do the ill effects exist in your area only or are they more widespread? Explain if these are local, regional, or national problems.

c. Who regulates these industries and problems and how? Has there been progress in alleviating the problems? If so, where did the impetus come from?

Step 4 Describe the short- and long-term health effects of each issue studied.

a. Explain if these are local problems or more widespread.

b. Are any of these problems associated with **cancer clusters**, or "hot spots," where the disease rate is much higher than for the general population?

Step 5 The ninth environmental issue listed on the home page is Setting Environmental Priorities.

a. Go to that page and access the smallest region closest to your home.

b. Once you have selected a region, outline the highest health and ecological risks for that region. How widespread are the risks?

c. What can be done to correct these problems? Describe how you can personally help avoid these problems.

1-11 Effects of Gamma Radiation on Seed Growth

PURPOSE

➤ Conduct a controlled experiment on rates of seed germination and plant growth, comparing the rates for exposures to different levels of gamma irradiation

➤ Apply experimental results to related issues of commercial irradiation of food and seed products

Materials

- 8 paper cups (or other small disposable containers)
- 2 types of seeds (purchased from a supplier and irradiated at 3 exposures)

Procedure

Step 1 Prepare 8 containers for plantings seeds. You will likely be using rye grass and mung bean seeds because they germinate quickly. The seeds will have been exposed to gamma rays at 3 different exposures.

Step 2 Place your name on the containers with a grease pencil or marker pen. Identify the containers: 3 rye grass, 3 mung bean, and 1 control for each seed type.

Step 3 With a pencil, poke a few small holes in the bottom of the containers for drainage. Fill the containers ¾ full of potting soil.

Step 4 Place five seeds in each cup and cover them with a little of the potting soil. Water the containers and place them in a warm lighted place for a week.

Step 5 Design a table of data to record your observations over the time period you run the experiment. Record when the plants first break the surface and how much they grow each day. Also record any changes in physical appearance from each other and the controls.

Step 6 Plot graphs of the average growth rate for each seed type and irradiation level.

Step 7 Plot the percent germination against the irradiation levels for each seed type.

Step 8 Draw conclusions about the percent germination, rate of growth, and appearance of plants, compared to the levels of irradiation.

Step 9 The U.S. Department of Agriculture and the Food and Drug Administration now accept the use of food irradiation as the most effective and efficient way of preventing microbiological contamination.

   a. Describe how your experiment could be modified and used to model a current world problem.

   b. Explain how the irradiation of seeds can be a useful process for the farm and garden industries.

   c. What are some environmental, social, and economical drawbacks of irradiating?

Step 10 Comment on the safety of using irradiated seeds.

   a. Why, after being bombarded with powerful gamma rays, are the seeds not radioactive?

   b. Why are irradiated foods safe to eat, despite some public fears?

Step 11 Extension For an even longer-term study, continue to grow the surviving plants until they produce their own seeds.

   a. Test the second generation plants using the same techniques as above.

   b. What differences in results do you observe?

The Rock Cycle, Rocks, and Soil

PURPOSE

➤ Collect local samples of igneous, sedimentary, and metamorphic rock to analyze and categorize

➤ Compare rock samples with surrounding soil samples to reach conclusions on local soil formation

Materials

- 25–50 rock samples

- corresponding soil samples

- 100-mL graduated cylinder

- hand lens

Alternative:
- rock and mineral kit

Fig. 1-9

The surface of Earth is constantly changing, most of the time too slowly to notice. The three rock types in the Rock Cycle have two main sources: sediments from erosion, and magma, a hot, natural melt composed mostly of steam and silicates from deep in the Earth.

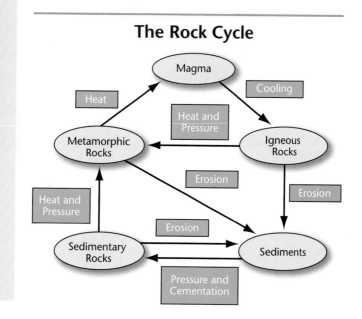

The Rock Cycle

Procedure

Step 1 Collect 25–50 different kinds of rocks from your neighborhood or the region around your home and school. The samples should be obviously different. (If you live in an area where this is impossible, use a rock and mineral kit from your science department.)

Step 2 If you collect the rocks yourself, also collect a small bag of soil from each area where you take samples.

Step 3 As best you can, group your samples into **igneous**, **metamorphic**, and **sedimentary** types.

Step 4 Define what is meant by igneous rocks.

    a. What is their source?

    b. Some igneous rocks are **intrusive** and others are **extrusive**. What does this mean, and how can you tell which type your samples are?

Fig. 1-10: **Granite Face of El Capitan at Yosemite National Park**

    c. What is meant by rock **texture**? Categorize your igneous rocks by texture.

    d. Use a hand lens to examine the size of the crystals in your samples. Are they uniform in size and are they evenly distributed throughout the sample? Compare all the igneous rocks this way.

    e. Are the rocks hard, brittle, or easily broken? For example, how would you categorize obsidian?

    f. What is the **Bowen's Series**? Describe how the properties of the rocks change based on the arrangement of silica tetrahedrons.

    g. From your knowledge of the Soil Triangle, what type of soils would your igneous rocks form? Does your soil sample bear this out? Why or why not?

Step 5 Define sedimentary rocks.

    a. Where do these rocks come from?

    b. Use a hand lens to describe the texture of your sedimentary rock samples.

    c. Try to determine the source of the grains in your sample. Are they angular, somewhat rounded, or well-rounded? Did they form in water or on dry land?

    d. Some sedimentary rocks have biological origins, such as coal and fossiliferous limestone; some are derived from inorganic chemicals like salt and gypsum; and some are made of other rock fragments. Categorize your samples. What can you tell of their origins?

Laboratory Investigations for AP Environmental Science

Fig. 1-11: Sedimentary Rocks on the Island of Cyprus

e. Only sedimentary rocks can have fossils. Describe any fossils that you find. What can you learn from them?

f. From your knowledge of the Soil Triangle, what type of soils can you expect from your samples? Will they form easily?

Step 6 Define metamorphic rocks.

a. How are they categorized?

b. Are your metamorphic samples caused by contact, hydrothermal, or regional metamorphism? How can you tell?

c. Describe some common metamorphic rocks by texture. Identify your samples in this manner.

d. How do heat and pressure play a role in the formation of your metamorphic samples? What clues do these factors give us about the geology at the time of their formation?

e. Describe how metamorphic rocks are useful to humans.

Fig. 1-12: Folded Metamorphic Rocks, Westchester County, NY

Step 7 Soils are made up of inorganic minerals, organic matter, water, and air. The minerals may be sorted by size and classified as sand, silt, or clay. The size of the particles is determined by several factors, including hardness of the original minerals, geologic processes that they may have been exposed to, atmospheric weathering, human pollution, and others.

a. Using a hand lens, examine the soil you collected along with your rock samples. Draw the mineral components as best you can.

b. Separate your soil into three size components by placing about 50 mL of soil in a graduated cylinder and filling it to the 75–80 mL mark with water. Shake up the cylinder with your hand over its mouth. Let it settle overnight and then separate the components.

c. Compare the grains of sand, silt, and clay to the components of your rock samples. How do they match up? What processes do you think were involved in the forming of the soil?

INVESTIGATION

2

Plate Tectonics

PURPOSE

➤ Plot key geologic events and correlate them to tectonic plate boundaries

INTRODUCTION

In the 1960s and 1970s it was becoming obvious that the map of Earth's continents has been continuously changing over a large portion of geologic history.

Fig. 2-1

Earth's Continents Over Last 225 Million Years

The theory of plate tectonics explains the drift of continents and related geological events.

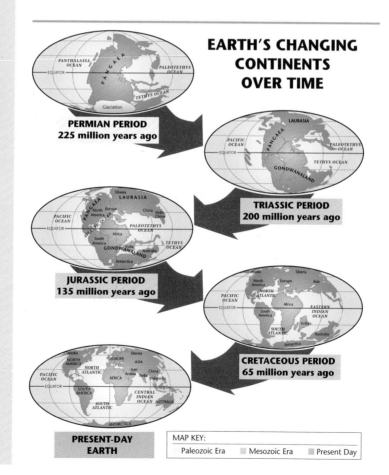

EARTH'S CHANGING CONTINENTS OVER TIME

PERMIAN PERIOD
225 million years ago

TRIASSIC PERIOD
200 million years ago

JURASSIC PERIOD
135 million years ago

CRETACEOUS PERIOD
65 million years ago

PRESENT-DAY EARTH

MAP KEY:
Paleozoic Era ▨ Mesozoic Era ▨ Present Day

Continental land masses crashed into and moved away from each other for over 2.0 billion years. These movements can be inferred from present-day geologic features resulting from these collisions and breakups. Rocks and fossils found in western Africa are also found in eastern South America. And scratches left on rocks by moving glaciers suggest how continents have moved over the last 300 million years.

The idea of drifting continents was first proposed in 1912 by Alfred Wegener, who observed that the continents seem to fit together like the pieces of a puzzle. Although the evidence suggested that Wegener was correct, he could not find a mechanism to explain how whole continents could move thousands of miles across the Earth's surface.

It is now believed that the continents move on pieces of the Earth's crust called **tectonic plates**. The surface of the Earth seems to be divided into seven or eight major plates and maybe a dozen smaller ones. The best explanation for the mechanism is that heat escaping from the planet's interior creates convection currents that move the plates into and away from each other. From a geological point of view, the most interesting places are the plate boundaries where the plates collide, separate, or slide past each other. Scientists infer the size, shape, and location of the plates by a process similar to the one you will undertake in this project.

In this investigation you will plot the locations of recent earthquakes, volcanic eruptions, and mountain ranges on a world map (see **Fig. 2-2**). These events are not evenly distributed over the Earth. You will be asked to look for patterns in the locations of these occurrences globally and discuss how they affect the planet and its inhabitants.

Procedure

Step 1   Go to the following Internet site:
http://neic.usgs.gov/neis/bulletin/
Using small circles as markers, mark on the world map the location of the 25 most recent earthquakes that are not in the same locale.

Step 2   Plot the location of the following volcanoes, using small triangles on the map.

Mt. Etna, Italy - 37.73N, 15.00E

Ayelu, Ethiopia - 10.082N, 40.702E

Likaiu, Kenya - 2.17N, 36.36E

White Island, New Zealand - 37.52S, 177.18E

Santorini, Greece - 36.4N, 25.4E

Askja, Iceland - 65.03N, 16.75W

El Chichon, Mexico - 17.4N, 93.2W

Mt. Wrangell, USA - 62.66N, 144.12W

Redoubt, USA - 60.5N, 152.7W

Mount Rainier, USA - 46.58N, 121.75W

Lassen Peak, USA - 40.5N, 121.5W

Unimak Island, USA - 54.47N, 163.9W

Mt. Pelee, West Indies - 14.8N, 61.1W

Blup Blup, Papua New Guinea - 3.5S,144.6E

Pinatubo, Philippines - 15.13N, 120.35E

Tambora, Indonesia - 8.3S, 118.0E

Gamalama, Indonesia - 0.8N, 127.3E

Irazu, Costa Rica - 9.979N, 83.853W

Lascar, Chile - 23.32S, 67.44W

Nevado del Ruiz, Columbia - 4.9N, 75.3W

Krasheninnikov, Russia - 54.58N, 160.26E

Fuji, Japan - 35.4N, 138.7E

Chaine des Puys, France - 45.5N, 2.8E

Soufriere Hills, Montserrat - 16.7N, 62.2W

Ararat, Turkey - 39.70 N, 44.28 E

Savo, Solomon Islands - 9.1S, 159.8E

Step 3 Again, using the map, shade in locations for the following mountain ranges.

Alps	California Coast Ranges	Karakoram
Andes	Carpathians	Mid Ocean Ridges
Appalachians	Cascades	Scandinavian Mts.
Atlas	Dolomites	Sierra Nevada
Balkin Mts.	Himalaya	Urals

Fig. 2-2

World Map

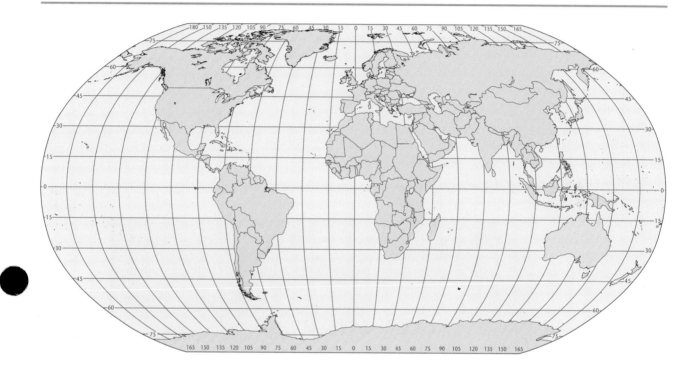

Questions

Exercises Problems Analysis

1a. What patterns do you observe in the locations of these earthquakes, volcanoes, and mountain ranges?

_____

_____

_____

_____

b. Why do these events seem common in some areas on Earth and rare in others?

_____

_____

_____

c. Using **Fig. 2-3**, compare your plotted positions with plate boundary locations. Describe any correlations.

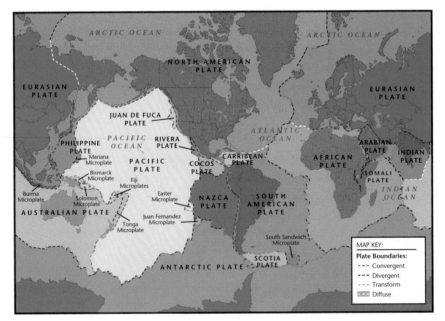

Fig. 2-3: **Earth's Plate Boundaries**

_____

_____

_____

_____

Laboratory Investigations for AP Environmental Science

d. How does the theory of Plate Tectonics explain these similarities of location? Describe how the theory of Plate Tectonics is strengthened by these patterns.

_____
_____
_____
_____
_____
_____

2. What is meant by the term *Ring of Fire*?

_____
_____
_____
_____
_____
_____

3a. How do the Ayelu and Likaiu volcanoes fit into the pattern you have observed?

_____
_____
_____
_____
_____

b. What processes are going on in eastern Africa? Explain what is meant by a *triple junction*.

_____
_____
_____
_____
_____
_____
_____

c. About two hundred million years ago a similar process occurred. (Refer back to **Fig. 2-1**, historical maps of Earth's drifting continents.) Describe this process.

_____

_____

_____

_____

_____

_____

_____

_____

4a. What are *hot spots*? Look at **Fig. 2-4**, showing a geological section of the Hawaiian Islands. What do hot spots tell us about plate movement?

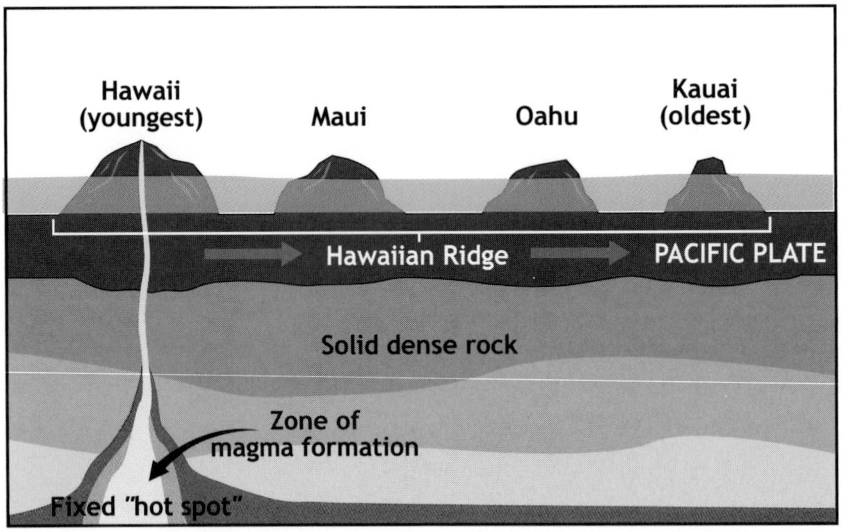

_____

_____

_____

_____

_____

_____

_____

Fig. 2-4: Geological Map of the Hawaiian Islands

b. Refer to **Fig. 2-5**. How has the hot spot in the Yellowstone region given clues about the movement of the North American Plate? Yellowstone National Park is in the upper right-hand corner of the image.

_____

_____

_____

_____

_____

_____

_____

_____

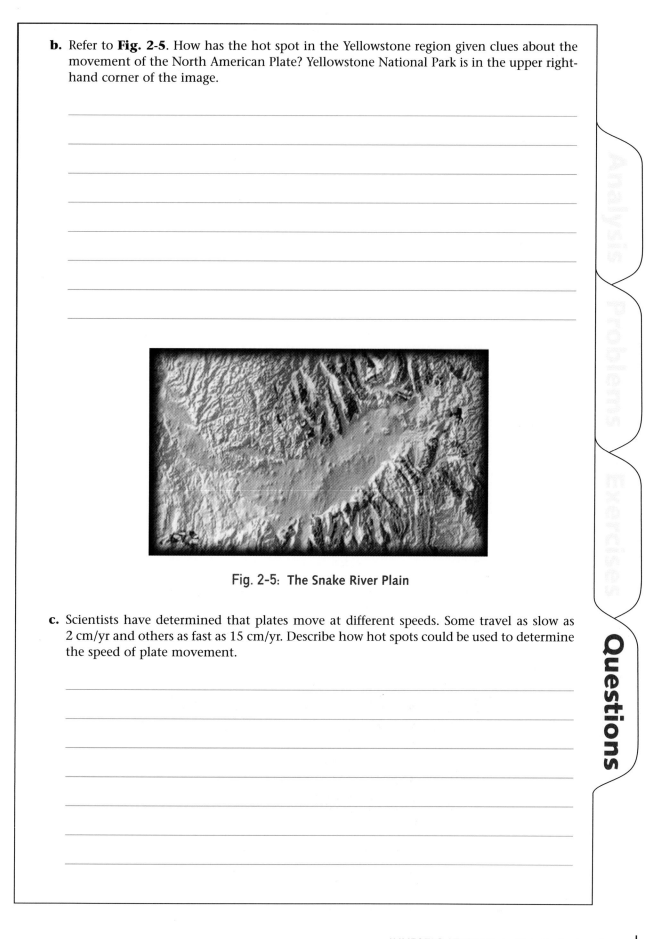

Fig. 2-5: **The Snake River Plain**

c. Scientists have determined that plates move at different speeds. Some travel as slow as 2 cm/yr and others as fast as 15 cm/yr. Describe how hot spots could be used to determine the speed of plate movement.

_____

_____

_____

_____

_____

_____

d. What information and measurements would you need to calculate the rate of movement?

_____

_____

_____

_____

_____

_____

5a. How did the Himalaya and Karakoram mountain ranges form? Twenty-two mountains in these mountain ranges are 8,000 m (26,240 ft) or higher, with Mt. Everest being the tallest on Earth at 8,850 m (29,028 ft). Why are these ranges so high even though they are not near a coast line?

_____

_____

_____

_____

_____

_____

b. Compare the Urals, another range in the list that is not near a continental edge, to the Himalaya and Karakoram. The highest mountain in the Urals is Naroda Mountain at 1,895 m (6,215 ft). Why are the Himalaya and Karakoram so much higher than the Urals?

_____

_____

_____

_____

_____

_____

_____

Specific Heat
and Climate

PURPOSE

➤ Determine the specific heat and the rates of heating of a soil sample, comparing them to those of water

➤ Relate specific heat findings to climatic phenomena

INTRODUCTION

The measure of the ability of a substance to change temperature is called **specific heat**. Some substances, such as air, change temperature with the addition of very little energy, while others need greater amounts of energy to change. The specific heat of a substance is defined as the heat needed to change the temperature of one gram of the substance one degree Celsius. For this exercise you will use the **Joule** (abbreviation **J**) as the unit of heat. (Other units of heat are the calorie and the BTU: one calorie is equal to 4.18 J and one BTU is equal to 1,055 J.) The more Joules needed for each degree change of a substance, the higher its specific heat.

Each substance has its own value for specific heat and these values can be found in many handbooks of science data. For example, iron has a value of 0.448 J/g °C. Many metals follow a general rule that their specific heat is approximately equal to 24.94/atomic weight. Ethanol, by contrast to iron, has a value of 2.43 J/g °C. So it takes about five times more energy to change the temperature of one gram of ethanol than to change the temperature of an equal mass of iron.

In this lab, you will determine the specific heat of a soil sample as compared to that of water. This difference has many ramifications regarding our climate, both local and global.

Materials

- 2 petri dishes
- soil
- water
- 2 thermometers
- heat lamp

Procedure

Step 1 In this lab, as in many of the investigations that follow, you will prepare tables to record and organize your experimental results. See **Fig. 3-2** on the following page for guidance in designing appropriate data tables for this lab.

Step 2 Record the mass of a petri dish and then add enough soil to fill it to the brim. Record the mass again. The difference is the mass of the soil sample.

Step 3 Record the mass of another petri dish and fill it with water. Record the mass again. The difference is the mass of the water.

Step 4 Place the thermometers so that the bulb of one is beneath the surface of the soil and the bulb of the other is under the water.

Step 5 Place both samples under a heat lamp, making sure the thermometers stay under the samples. Bring the lamp close to the petri dishes so that they are heated equally.

Step 6 Record the temperature of each thermometer every 30 seconds, for 10 minutes.

Step 7 Graph your temperature data on the same set of coordinates.

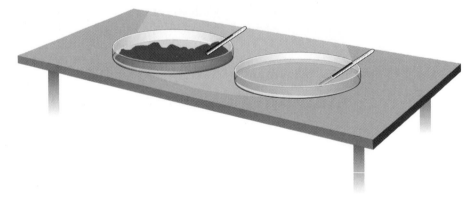

Fig. 3-1

MASS / TEMPERATURE DATA

	Soil	Water
Mass of Petri Dish and Material		
Mass of Petri Dish Empty		
Mass of Material		
Initial Temperature		
Final Temperature		

TEMPERATURE READINGS
(Intervals of 30 Seconds)

Temp.			Temp.		
#	Soil	Water	#	Soil	Water
1			11		
2			12		
3			13		
4			14		
5			15		
6			16		
7			17		
8			18		
9			19		
10			20		

Fig. 3-2: Data Tables

1a. Which sample showed the greater change in total temperature?

_____

_____

_____

b. For each petri dish, calculate the change in temperature per gram of substance.

_____

_____

c. Which substance heated up faster? Which has the higher specific heat?

_____

_____

_____

d. What do you think the results would be if the experiment were designed to measure the cooling behavior of each material?

_____

_____

_____

2a. From your graph, what does the shape of the line tell you about rates of heating?

_____

_____

_____

b. Describe how you could predict the temperature of the soil and water after 15 minutes of heating. What would each temperature be?

_____

_____

_____

c. After 20 minutes of heating, what would be the temperature of each matter? How accurate would that prediction be? Why?

_____

_____

_____

d. What would be the specific heat of each material after 15 minutes of heating? Why?

_____

_____

_____

3a. The Earth is heated by the sun. Based on this investigation, how would land masses heat up compared to the sea at the same latitude? Explain.

_____

_____

_____

b. If air over the warmer area rises, creating a lower atmospheric pressure, how would surrounding air move?

_____

_____

_____

c. Explain how this factor causes cooling sea breezes on a sunny day on a coastal beach. How does this relate to large-scale atmospheric changes, such as the Asian Monsoon?

_____

_____

_____

_____

_____

_____

_____

4a. Using the results of this lab, reason out why the yearly temperature ranges of interior regions of the United States are much larger than yearly coastal temperature ranges.

_____

_____

_____

_____

b. Why is the average winter temperature in Anchorage, Alaska, similar to that of New York City (about 1,700 miles south; about 20° of latitude closer to the Equator), while Fairbanks, Alaska, just 300 miles north of Anchorage, is 20–50 degrees colder than Anchorage?

_____

_____

_____

c. Compare temperatures for London, England, and Moscow, Russia, separated by about 4° of latitude. Explain how this difference could be explained partly by the same factors.

_____

_____

_____

5a. If the specific heat of water is 4.18 J/g °C, calculate the heat gained by the water.

Heat = (mass of absorber substance)(change in temp.)(specific heat)
In symbolic form: $q = m \, \Delta t \, c$

b. If the total heat gained by the water is about the same as the heat gained by the soil, calculate the specific heat of the soil.

Heat gain by **water** = Heat gain by **soil**
$m \, \Delta t \, c = m \, \Delta t \, c$

c. How does the specific heat of the soil relate to your answers in question 4?

_____

_____

_____

_____

_____

_____

_____

INVESTIGATION

4

Formation *of* Deserts

PURPOSE

➤ Explain factors in the existence and location of Earth's deserts

➤ Analyze atmospheric, geographic, and oceanographic data in relation to desert formation

BACKGROUND

Why are there deserts and why do they exist where they do? **Deserts** are geographic places that receive less than 25 cm, or 10 in., of rain each year. They usually are found in areas where moisture-laden air fails to come in contact with the land. Many deserts are hot in the daytime and cold at night. It is not uncommon for their temperature to change as much as 50°F from day to night. This is primarily because of their low humidity, between 10–20%. By contrast, deciduous forests in the eastern United States, with about 80% humidity during the day, absorb heat and hold much of it during the night. There the average temperature change in summer is only about 20°F from day to night. Water has a high **heat capacity**, as you learned in Investigation 3, and must lose a lot of energy for a small temperature change, whereas soils can change temperature quickly. For this reason water vapor is a very effective greenhouse gas.

Fig. 4-1

"The Mittens," Mesas on the Navajo Indian Reservation in Arizona's Monument Valley

While deserts cover 20% of the Earth's surface, they are not randomly distributed. And not all deserts are hot. They can exist in cold regions as well, provided they lack precipitation. Below are examples of how this phenomenon explains the existence of most of the world's deserts, which exist generally in four types of regions.

I. **High-Pressure Areas** Many people who watch TV weather reports know that low pressure generally means rainy, damp conditions while high pressure brings dry, clear weather. The same rules apply to geographic regions. Belts of high pressure around Earth, near the latitudes of 30°N and 30°S, seem to correspond to many of the world's hot deserts. High-pressure zones also occur at the poles, which are cold deserts.

II. **Mountain Areas** Mountain ranges tend to remove water from the atmosphere as air masses rise to move across the range, from **windward** to **leeward**, leaving much drier air to descend on the other side. Deserts can form on the downwind, or leeward, side of the mountain range. These are sometimes called **rainshadow deserts**.

III. **Coastal Areas** Some deserts are coastal, a fact that might seem to contradict the lack of moisture rule for deserts. Atmospheric moisture comes from the sea—remember the **Hydrologic Cycle**. The air over the ocean may be nearly saturated with water, but the total amount of water depends on the water temperature. Cold coastal water does not evaporate easily and can even remove atmospheric moisture. Cold air holds less moisture. When this cold, low-humidity air moves onto land that is warmer than the ocean, the air warms and absorbs moisture from the land, making it drier than it would normally be.

IV. **Inland Areas** The interiors of large continental land masses are usually much drier than the coasts. Moist air from off-shore usually loses much of its water by the time it reaches the interior.

Fig. 4-2

Earth's Desert Regions

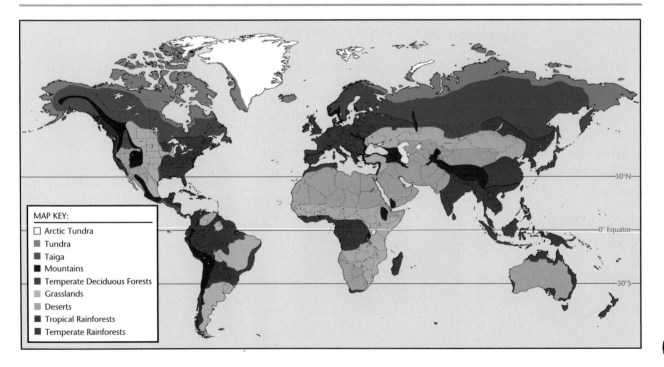

MAP KEY:
☐ Arctic Tundra
■ Tundra
■ Taiga
■ Mountains
■ Temperate Deciduous Forests
■ Grasslands
■ Deserts
■ Tropical Rainforests
■ Temperate Rainforests

1. Explain why there are global high-pressure and low-pressure belts on Earth. In some detail, tell how the high-pressure belts give rise to many of the world's largest deserts.

_____

_____

_____

_____

_____

_____

_____

_____

2. For this question, use your text or other sources as needed. Then, on the drawing of the globe, **Fig. 4-3**, draw and label:

   a. The major high- and low-pressure belts of Earth

   b. The following wind belts, indicating with arrows the direction in which they blow:

   - Doldrums
   - Tropical Easterlies (tradewinds)
   - Horse Latitudes
   - Prevailing Westerlies
   - Polar Easterlies

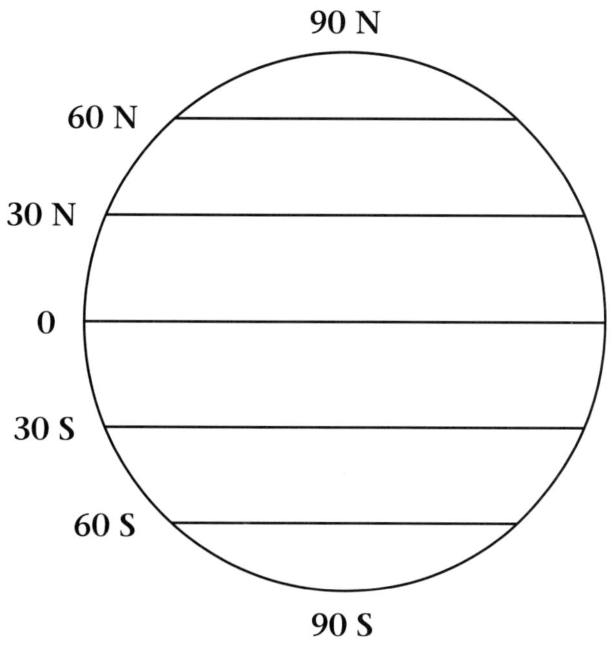

Fig. 4-3: **Earth's Major Wind and Pressure Belts**

3. Based on the information you drew on the map for Question 2 and your knowledge of the major mountain ranges of North and South America, explain the following:

a. the deserts of eastern Washington State and Oregon

_____

_____

b. the deserts of Nevada, Utah, and Arizona

_____

_____

c. Death Valley of California

_____

_____

d. the Atacama Desert of Chile on the western side of the Andes and the Monte Desert of Argentina on the eastern side of the Andes

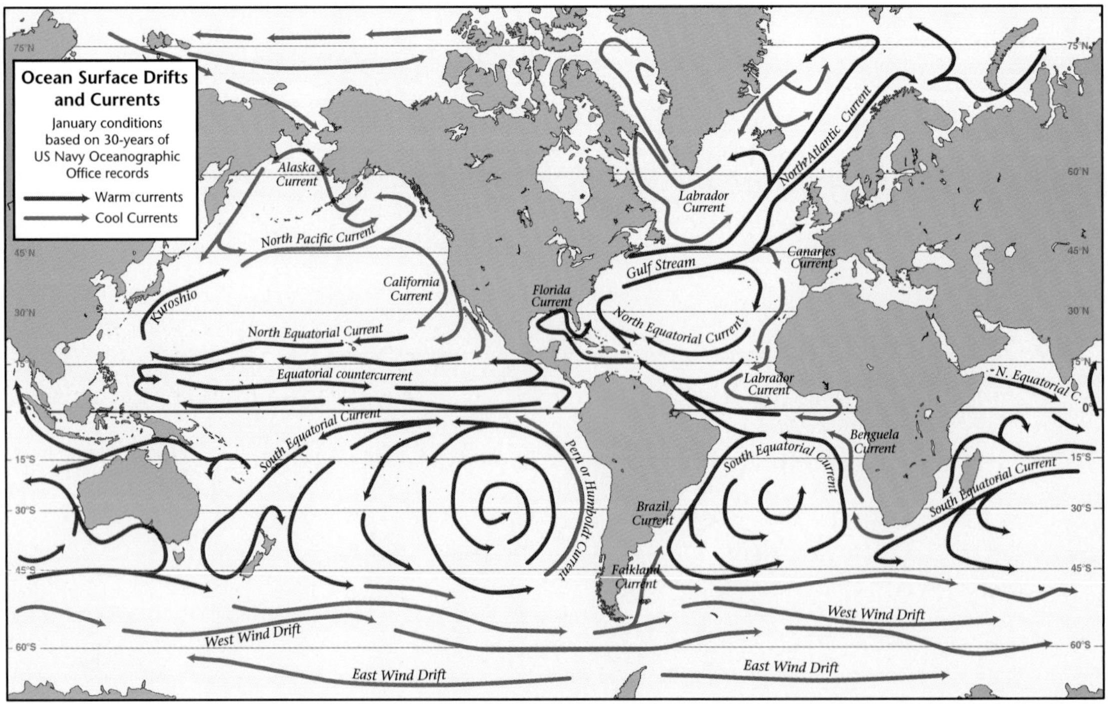

_____

_____

_____

Fig. 4-4: Major Ocean Currents

Laboratory Investigations for AP Environmental Science

4. Observe in **Fig. 4-4** the major surface currents of the Earth's oceans. The large circulations are called **gyres** by oceanographers. In the northern hemisphere the gyres move clockwise and in the southern oceans counterclockwise. Notice that some currents, such as the Peru current, move from the poles toward the Equator, bringing cold water along the coast. Others, like the Gulf Stream on the east coast of the United States, bring warm water from the tropics.

a. Should the east coast of South Africa be drier than the west coast of the country? Why or why not?

_____

_____

_____

_____

_____

_____

b. Explain how the cold California Current contributes to the dryness of southern California, Arizona, and New Mexico.

_____

_____

_____

_____

_____

_____

_____

5. Why is there a large desert region in central Asia, while the central plains of the interior United States is not a desert? As part of your answer, describe the differences between the geography of central Asia, with its relation to the Indian Ocean, and the central plains of the United States, with its proximity to the Gulf of Mexico.

_____

_____

_____

_____

_____

6. Briefly describe how rising and sinking air (high and low pressure) in the atmosphere can be the same explanation for:

a. clear and rainy days

_____

_____

b. deserts near 30° N and 30° S

_____

_____

c. rain shadows

_____

_____

_____

_____

d. the Monsoon of southern Asia and the southwestern United States

_____

_____

_____

_____

7. Describe three strategies or adaptations used by the following to survive in desert environments:

a. plants

_____

_____

_____

_____

b. vertebrate animals

_____

_____

_____

_____

INVESTIGATION

5

Natural Areas

PURPOSE

➤ Research and describe the history, ecosystems, species, and natural importance of a protected area in the United States

INTRODUCTION

In the time after the American Civil War, most people in the United States thought that our country was almost limitless in the amount of land and resources we possessed. Even so, there was a growing conservation movement that sought to put aside places of spectacular beauty, protect them from exploitation, and preserve them for future generations. In the late 1860s government surveyors started to map the West, taking with them photographers and artists to record the land they were mapping. Some of their works inspired Congress in 1872 to set aside what is now Yellowstone National Park. This was the first national park on Earth. Since then, many others have been added here and elsewhere around the globe. In the United States today there are many designations of protected land, based on their degree of protection. Over 40 million hectares (102 million acres) of wilderness are governed by four federal agencies.

The original objective of the national parks was to preserve the beauty of the various sites for the recreational use of the people. The mission has since broadened to include biological conservation. In national parks it is forbidden, for example, to pick flowers, collect rocks, and gather dead wood from the ground for campfires. The goal is to leave the natural balance of nature

Fig. 5-1

Emblems of U.S. Agencies Entrusted with Protection of Wilderness Areas

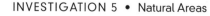

undisturbed. Recently, there has also been an emphasis on scientific research to protect, not only the land, but the organisms and their whole habitat. This is sometimes a difficult task because the park boundaries were established long before we were knowledgeable of ecosystems. The Yellowstone ecosystem is about twice as large as the park itself. It is not possible to protect all the wildlife that wanders outside the park boundary as part of their normal behavior. In Montana, for example, it is legal to hunt grazing buffalo as they cross the line from the protection of park.

Procedure

To complete this project, you and a partner will research and write a paper of about 800 to 1,000 words. You will select one region of our country and describe:

Step 1 Geological origins of the region

Step 2 Natural history: biome, climate, wildlife

Step 3 Type of ecosystem and which endangered species this ecosystem protects

Step 4 Characteristics of the area that make it important to preserve

Step 5 Effects this area had on human history and why it is unique and important to preserve from that perspective

Step 6 What agency is responsible for protection of the area

Step 7 Threats to the area's existence or mission to preserve and some ways to alleviate these threats

You will also need to present:

Step 8 Charts, diagrams, and/or maps to illustrate your findings

To choose a region, review the two tables that follow. The first lists National Parks, Monuments, Reserves, Seashores, and Recreation Areas for possible areas. A second list offers other possibilities for areas of unique natural interest that are not protected by a federal agency. If you wish to choose an area not on either list, consult with your teacher for permission.

As you prepare your report, keep in mind that your instructor will evaluate your work based on criteria like the following:

Scoring Rubric

- Neatness, organization and bibliography   10%
- Clear explanation of geologic and natural history   30%
- Human history and value   25%
- Threats to area's existence and possible cures   25%
- Charts, diagrams, pictures, maps, etc.   10%

Table 5-1

Federally Protected Natural Areas in the United States

Area	State	Area	State
Acadia NP	Maine	Rocky Mountain NP	Colorado
Arches NP	Utah	Sequoia NP	California
Arctic National WR	Alaska	Saguaro NP	Arizona
Badlands NP	South Dakota	Shenandoah NP	Virginia
Big Bend NP	Texas	Theodore Roosevelt NP	North Dakota
Biscayne NP	Florida	Virgin Islands NP	Virgin Islands
Black Canyon of the Gunnison NP	Colorado	Voyageurs NP	Minnesota
		Wind Cave NP	South Dakota
Bryce Canyon NP	Utah	Wrangell-St. Elias NP	Alaska
Capitol Reef NP	Utah	Yellowstone NP	Wyoming
Carlsbad Caverns NP	New Mexico	Yosemite NP	California
Channel Islands NP	California	Zion NP	Utah
Crater Lake NP	Oregon	Canyon De Chelley NM	Arizona
Death Valley NP	California	Capulin Mountain NM	New Mexico
Denali NP	Alaska	Cedar Breaks NM	Utah
Everglades NP	Florida	Chiricahua NM	Arizona
Gates of the Arctic NP	Alaska	Colorado NM	Colorado
Glacier NP	Montana	Craters of the Moon NM	Idaho
Glacier Bay NP	Alaska	Devils Postpile NM	California
Grand Canyon NP	Arizona	Devils Tower NM	Wyoming
Grand Teton NP	Wyoming	Florissant Fossil Beds NM	Colorado
Great Basin NP	Nevada	Fossil Butte NM	Wyoming
Great Smokey Mountain NP	North Carolina	Grand Staircase- Escalante NM	Utah
Guadalupe Mountain NP	Texas	Great Sand Dunes NM	Colorado
Joshua Tree NP	California	Jewel Cave NM	South Dakota
Haleakala NP	Hawaii	Lava Beds NM	California
Hawaii Volcano NP	Hawaii	Misty Fjords NM	Alaska
Hot Springs NP	Arkansas	Mt. St. Helens NM	Washington
Isle Royale NP	Michigan	Mohave Nat Preserve	California
Katmai NP	Alaska	Natural Bridges NM	Utah
Kenai Fjords NP	Alaska	Pinnacles NM	California
Kings Canyon NP	California	Rainbow Bridge NM	Utah
Kobuk Valley NP	Alaska	Sunset Crater NM	Arizona
Lake Clark NP	Alaska	Timpanogos Cave NM	Utah
Lassen Peak NP	California	White Sands NM	New Mexico
Mammoth Cave NP	Kentucky	New Jersey Pinelands NR	New Jersey
Mesa Verde NP	Colorado	Cape Cod NRA	Massachusetts
Mt. Ranier NP	Washington	Delaware Water Gap NRA	NJ, PA
Northern Cascades NP	Washington	Gateway NRA	NY, NJ
Olympic NP	Washington	Lake Mead NRA	Utah
Petrified Forest NP	Arizona	Lake Powell NRA	Utah
Redwood NP	California	Padre Island NS	Texas

Table 5-2

Important Natural Areas in the United States Not Federally Protected

Area	State	Area	State
Adirondack Mountains	New York	Great Lakes	U.S., Canada
Barrier Islands	East Coast	Great Salt Lake	Utah
Bonneville Salt Flats	Utah	Hackensack	
Cape Cod	Massachusetts	Meadowlands	New Jersey
Colorado Plateau	CO, AR, UT, NM	Long Island	New York
Columbia Plateau	WA, OR	Permian Basin	Texas

Fig. 5-2

The Florida Everglades

The Moon *and* Tides

Project

PURPOSE

➤ Find, organize, graph, and analyze tide data for one month
➤ Track and graph the relative positions of Earth, the moon, and the sun for the same month
➤ Explain the occurrence and heights of the tides in view of the motions of these bodies

PART I

BACKGROUND

For thousands of years humans have recognized the effect the moon has on the changing water levels you observe at the beach. Winds and ocean currents cause waves, but the periodic changing of water level we call tides is more complex. Tides vary from day to day, based on the relative positions of Earth, the moon, and the sun in space. On most coastlines there are two high and two low tides per twenty-five hour period. These are called **semidiurnal tides**.

Fig. 6-1

Low tide occurs as the Earth rotates out of the tidal bulge.

The gravitational effect of the moon and sun are the major cause of tidal variation, but other factors also are an influence. The Gulf of Mexico has **diurnal tides**, or only one high and one low tide per twenty-five hour period, because the Gulf of Mexico is not an open body of water, but semi-enclosed. Mexico's coastline blocks the in-and-out flow of water that normally causes two high and two low tides in the same period.

In this project you will use the Internet to examine more closely the water level patterns that exist at a particular location. You will investigate a probable cause and effect relationship between the moon and the regular variation in water level.

Procedure

Step 1 You and your partner will use the Internet to find tide data for one month. Any location along our coastline is acceptable. You may find this Web site helpful:

http://tidesonline.nos.noaa.gov/

Set your parameters as follows (Sandy Hook, in northern New Jersey, is used as an example):

Station: 8531680 Sandy Hook, NJ (or any other you may select)
Tide interval: W3 High/Lows
Datum: MLLW (for distance above **M**ean **L**ower **L**ow **W**ater)
Begin Date: 20041101
End Date: 20041130
Time: LST (for Local Standard Time)
Data Units: meters (1 m = 3.28 ft)

Then press View Data

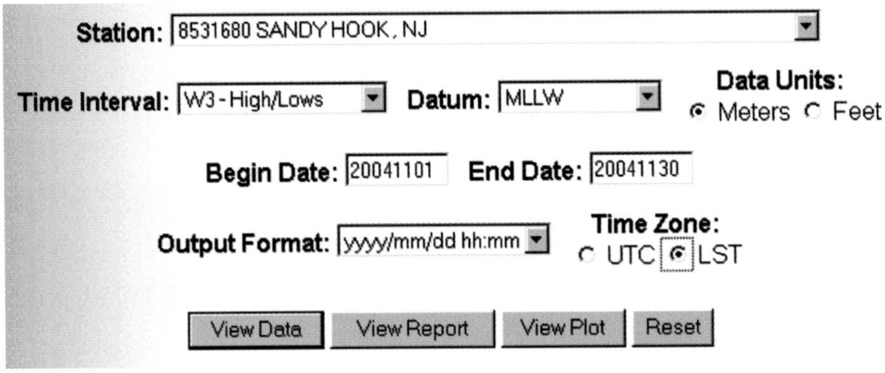

Fig. 6-2: **Data Entry Field at National Ocean Service Web Site**

Step 2 On a data sheet that you will organize, enter the heights of all the high and low tides for the month, in order. (As an option, you might print out the data from the Web site, then enter the data into a spreadsheet to make analysis easier.)

Step 3 Prepare a graph with time along the horizontal axis and the heights along the vertical axis. To make the horizontal scale simple to read, number the high and low tides from the first to the last day of the month.

Let your data determine the intervals of the vertical scale, also making allowances for possible negative values. In making a graph you want to spread the data out over most of the graph paper, so set your scales accordingly.

Step 4 Plot your data. Connect the high tide marks with a smooth, best-fitting line. Do the same for the low-tide data.

1a. What general patterns do you observe?

_____

_____

_____

_____

_____

b. How do the high-tide data vary over the month? Are all high tides equally high? Why or why not? Explain.

_____

_____

_____

_____

_____

c. How do the low-tide data vary over the same time period? Are all low tides equally low? Why or why not? Explain.

_____

_____

_____

_____

_____

d. Define and explain *spring tide* and *neap tide*.

_____

_____

_____

_____

_____

_____

e. Are the high tides on the same day of equal heights? What about the low-tide heights on the same day? What could explain such observations?

_____

_____

_____

_____

_____

_____

_____

_____

_____

2. Compare the variation of the high-tide data and the low-tide data relative to each other over the month. Why do the high points on one curve occur during the low points on the other?

_____

_____

_____

_____

_____

_____

_____

_____

_____

_____

3. Compare your data with those of another group who used a different site and/or month. Describe and explain the similarities and differences.

_____

_____

_____

_____

_____

_____

_____

_____

4. Give two examples of why is it important, from a biological point of view, to understand the tides.

_____

_____

_____

_____

_____

_____

_____

5. There are trillions of watts of energy produced by the tides. Doing research as necessary, describe one method that might be developed to harness that energy for use by humans.

_____

_____

_____

_____

_____

_____

_____

_____

Problems

Exercises

Questions

PART II

BACKGROUND

The moon has apparent phases because of where we stand on Earth and how much of its face we see illuminated. The sun continuously lights up one full side of the moon, but that side is not always visible from our vantage point on Earth

as the moon revolves in its 27.3 day orbit around our planet. This 27.3 day period is called the **sidereal month** and is the true orbital period. The phase cycle takes a bit longer to complete because Earth also is moving in an orbital path around the sun. The phase cycle is the **synodic month** and it is 29.5 days long.

The phases of the moon do not cause the variation in the tides; the positions of the moon and sun with respect to Earth do. The phases are a visual way to keep track of the positions of these bodies.

Fig. 6-3

The Moon in Full Phase

Procedure

Step 1   Use the following Web site to find the phases of the moon for the month for which you have collected tide data:
http://aa.usno.navy.mil/data/docs/MoonPhase.html

Step 2   Record on your graph the days on which the various moon phases occurred.

Step 3   In the space below, draw how Earth, the moon, and the sun would be relatively positioned for each phase.

6. How do you think the combined gravity of the sun and moon and the rotation of the Earth influence the height of the oceans?

_____

_____

_____

_____

_____

7. From your sketches and the data on your graphs, draw some conclusions:

a. Why are there high and low tides?

_____

_____

_____

b. Why are there usually two high and two low tides each day in most places?

_____

_____

_____

c. Why do the heights of the high and low tides fluctuate over time?

_____

_____

_____

d. From what you know about the orbit of the moon around Earth, explain why the high tides do not occur at the same time each day.

_____

_____

_____

Analysis

8. The moon presently is about 239,000 miles away, on the average, and takes a little over 27 days to complete one orbit of Earth. About 900,000 years ago the moon was only about 200,000 miles away and it took about 20 days for one orbit. Geologic and astronomical evidence suggest that the moon has been moving away at a steady rate of about 3.82 cm/yr (1.5 inches per year). Earth and the moon are gravitationally connected and because of that Earth's rotation has slowed down over the same time period from 18 hour days to the present 24 hours. This means that 900,000 years ago the year was 481 days long.

   a. Why is the length of the day lengthening as the moon's orbit expands?

   b. Describe how the tides would vary under the conditions of 900,000 years ago.

   c. Outline two ways the day-night cycle and the tidal variations affect life on Earth.

Lab

Copper Extraction

PURPOSE

➤ Measure the amount of copper metal you can extract from copper (II) carbonate, the main ingredient in the mineral malachite

➤ Model an environmentally sound, modern method of extracting copper profitably from tailings

INTRODUCTION

Most metals are found in Earth combined with other elements. The term **ore** is used to describe a piece of Earth's crust that contains profitable amounts of a metal. Malachite is an ore that is common in the Southwest of the United States and is a form of copper (II) carbonate, with the formula $CuCO_3Cu(OH)_2$. The green corrosion that forms on copper due to weathering, such as seen on the Statue of Liberty, has the same composition as malachite. The reactions of malachite are similar to those of copper (II) carbonate.

Commercial copper mining has gone on in many regions of the United States for over 100 years. Most of the copper mines use the open pit method of extracting ore. In the early days the technology for extracting metal from the ore was

Fig. 7-1

Open Pit Copper Mine

crude. To yield salable amounts of metal, the ore had to be at least 2.5% copper by mass. A lot of copper was left behind in the residue, or **tailing piles**, because the technology was not able to remove it profitably. As time went on, our technology improved, and profitable amounts of copper were taken from lower grade ores. By the year 2000, American miners were making a profit on ore that was 0.44% copper. Old tailing piles that accumulated around the mines still had valuable copper in them, but it was easier and cheaper to dig new ore out of the ground and process that for the metal, both here and overseas.

From an environmental point of view, the old tailing piles are a major contributor to water pollution. Many copper ores contain sulfides, which, mixed with water become strongly acidic. These acid waters can then leach metals out of the waste piles, making the run-off water even more toxic. This problem is especially severe in arid regions where water is already at a premium. In many areas of the West the mines and their tailings were abandoned as the price of copper fell and offshore sources became cheaper, but the pollution remained.

In the last 15 to 20 years a few small companies have developed processes to remove profitable amounts of copper from the old tailing piles. This practice helps revitalize the local economy, removes some of the tailings, and improves water quality. In this lab, you will model methods used in the Southwest to reduce the tailing piles, clean up the environment, and, at the same time, turn a profit.

Fig. 7-2

Tailing Piles at an Open Pit Mine

Materials

- safety goggles
- dilute sulfuric acid
- wash bottle
- water, distilled
- copper (II) carbonate
- balance
- glass rod
- Bunsen burner
- iron filings
- 2 beakers, 250 mL
- filter paper
- funnel

Procedure

Step 1 Add 6 g of copper (II) carbonate to a dry beaker and add 10 mL distilled water.

Step 2 Carefully add 15 mL of 6M sulfuric acid. **WEAR EYE PROTECTION.**

Step 3 Heat gently and stir with a glass rod.

Step 4 Add 2.7 g of iron filings and stir until there is no more color change in the solution.

Step 5 Place your name on a clean, dry piece of filter paper and record its mass.

Step 6 With the wash bottle, flush the liquid and solid from the bottom of the beaker into the folded filter paper in a funnel. Be sure to rinse all the solid into the filter. Allow the solution to drain fully into the beaker under the funnel and then rinse the filtrate with more distilled water.

Step 7 When all the water has drained through the filter, remove it from the funnel, then open it up carefully on a tray to dry overnight.

Step 8 During the next lab period, record the mass of the dry filter paper and filtrate. Measure the mass of copper collected.

Step 9 Calculate the percent yield, based on the expected amount of copper metal.

Data and Calculations

Step 10a Write the correct chemical equations for the reactions in this lab.

_____

_____

b Show your data table and measurements for your yield of copper.

_____

_____

_____

c Calculate your expected yield of copper from the balanced equation.

_____

_____

d How many grams of copper did you collect, compared to your expected yield? What was the percent yield in your experiment?

_____

_____

Read the questions below. Conduct independent research, if necessary, to respond fully.

1. From your research, describe how the method you modeled is used in the metal industry. How could it be used on a large scale?

_____

_____

_____

_____

_____

2. There are many other minerals mined in the United States and around the world that leave large tailing piles. Describe a method for cleaning tailing piles for a mineral other than copper.

_____

_____

_____

_____

_____

3. Explain how cyanide is used to mine gold. Why is this such a controversial method in the Northern Rocky Mountains? What environmental problems does this method present?

_____

_____

_____

_____

_____

4. Describe an alternate method of mining gold without the use of cyanide.

_____

_____

_____

_____

_____

INVESTIGATION 8

Energy *and* Recycling

PURPOSE

➤ Compare energy costs of recycling aluminum for cans to making cans from raw materials

➤ Investigate extrinsic benefits and disadvantages of recycling, such as environmental and economic factors

BACKGROUND

The county government in one eastern state initiated an aluminum recycling program. Most of the aluminum is in the form of beverage cans. In the first year, the county collected 1.4×10^6 kg of cans. It takes about 65 modern aluminum cans to make a kilogram.

All communities in the county have curb-side pickup of recycled materials. On average, each truck makes a 75-km trip to pick up 3,500 kg of aluminum and gets 5 km/L fuel economy. Each liter of fuel produces 42,000 kJ energy.

Fig. 8-1

Scrap Aluminum to Be Recycled

1. How many cans did the county collect in the first year?

2. To the nearest whole number, how many trips were needed to collect all the cans?

3. Calculate how many liters of fuel the trucks used to pick up the cans.

4. How many kilojoules (KJ) of energy were consumed collecting the cans?

5. Making cans from recycled aluminum requires about 180 kJ of energy per can. Calculate the total energy needed to make cans from recycled aluminum, including the energy used to collect them.

6. It takes 1,520 kJ of energy to make one aluminum can from bauxite ore. Assuming no other energy is used, calculate how much energy is needed to make the cans from bauxite ore.

7. Calculate the energy difference between the two methods. How many liters of fuel are saved by recycling the cans?

Apparently, there is a considerable energy savings in using recycled aluminum to make new cans. The decision to recycle is surely not that simple. There are many other factors to take into account.

8. Describe two environmental and two economic problems associated with the recycling of aluminum.

_____

_____

_____

_____

_____

_____

_____

_____

_____

_____

There are many materials that lend themselves to recycling. Some of these do not have the clear-cut, easy-to-see advantage of recycling aluminum. Take glass for example. To make glass from raw materials requires a little over 18,100 kJ/kg of glass manufactured. To make glass from recycled materials takes about 16,700 kJ/kg of glass product. If the costs of collecting the recycled glass are factored in, the energy savings are more than offset.

9. Cite two environmental and two economic reasons to manufacture glass from recycled materials, even if the costs are higher than from using raw materials.

_____

_____

_____

_____

_____

_____

_____

_____

_____

Paper or plastic? Since the 1980s grocery shoppers have had that choice. Many customers selected paper, correctly thinking that it is made of natural, renewable, environmentally friendly materials. The polyethylene plastic bags were made from nonrenewable crude oil. As usual, the choice is not as clear-cut as it seems.

10a. Compare the manufacture, use, and reuse potential of paper versus plastic grocery bags. Investigate the manufacture of each for:

air pollution	water pollution
solid waste	energy use
cost	land use

b. Other factors to consider:

landfill volume	ease of recycling
reuse	biodegradability

c. Explain two alternatives to paper or plastic grocery bags.

INVESTIGATION 9

Soil Analysis

PURPOSE

➤ Analyze a soil sample and remediate soil based on analysis

➤ Compare growth rate, taste, and other factors in crop samples from remediated and non-remediated soils

INTRODUCTION

Collect a soil sample by digging a small hole at least 12 inches deep. Remove any stones, roots, grass, or thatch from the sample and place in a one-gallon plastic sealable bag. Make notes on the surroundings where you collected your sample. Factors such as plant life, buildings, walkways, and paved areas may influence some of your tests and give clues about why you got the results you measured.

Materials

- local soil sample
- lettuce seeds
- hand lens
- 100-mL graduated cylinder
- 250-mL beaker
- centimeter ruler
- aluminum foil
- porcelain crucible
- drying oven
- ring stand and burner
- filter paper
- plastic bottles
- ethanol
- soil test kit (or CBL2)
- sample of clay
- sample of sand

Preliminary Investigation Two weeks prior to the start of this lab, put your name on a paper cup, and poke three holes in the bottom. Fill it with a sample of your soil and plant 5 to 10 lettuce seeds in it. Place the cup in warm sunlight and water it. Over the next two weeks care for your lettuce seeds as well as possible, recording your observations in a daily journal about how many seeds germinated and when, their growth rates, and appearance. Then begin the analysis of your sample using the following procedures.

 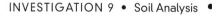

Take some of your sample and carefully place it on a tray or large piece of paper. Look closely at your soil sample. What do you see? Record the forms of organic matter, such as worms, insects, plant roots, etc. Observe and comment on the various particle sizes. Do any sizes dominate? Use a hand lens and draw what you see.

1. General Observations:

2. Abiotic components of your sample:

3. Biotic components of your sample:

Soil is made of mineral particles belonging to three size categories: clay, silt, and sand. The size of soil particles is important. Large particles of sand allow empty space for air and water to enter the soil. Smaller silt and clay particles help hold the water in a soil so that it does not drain away too quickly to be of use to plants. The ratios of these materials, or **texture**, can be determined qualitatively and quantitatively.

Qualitative Test Take a small moist wad of your sample and squeeze it between your thumb and forefinger. If it feels gritty, then you have mostly sand. If it feels sticky, then you have mostly clay. If it feels neither gritty nor sticky, then you have mostly silt.

If you can squeeze out a long, unbroken ribbon of soil from your fingers, you have clay. If you can squeeze out a short ribbon, you have silt or loam. If you cannot form a ribbon, then you have sand or sandy loam.

1. What type of soil do you think you have? Why?

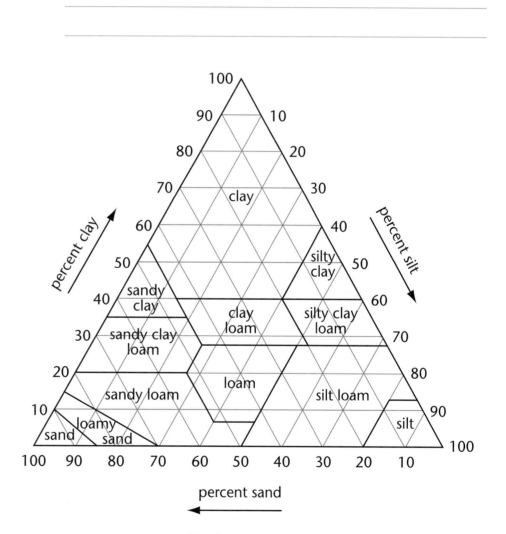

Fig. 9-1: Soil Triangle

Quantitative Test In a 100-mL graduated cylinder, place about 60–70 mL of your soil sample. Add enough water to saturate the soil completely and then keep adding water until the level gets to about the 100-mL mark. Now place your hand tightly over the open end of the graduated cylinder to seal it and shake the whole apparatus until the soil and water completely mix to make a free-moving slurry. Be sure to break up any lumps in the soil. Do this for at least one minute. Now place the graduated cylinder in a safe place for 24 hours, to let the soils settle out. The denser, large sand particles will settle out first and be on the bottom of the cylinder. A layer of silt will settle out on top of the sand and finally, after 12 to 24 hours, the tiny clay particles will settle out on top of the silt.

For calculations, show all setups with proper units.

2. With a centimeter ruler, measure the height of each layer and the total height of the sample. Calculate the percent of sand, silt, and clay in the sample.

   Total height: _____ cm, _____ %   Silt: _____ cm, _____ %

   Sand: _____ cm, _____ %   Clay: _____ cm, _____ %

3. What type of soil do you have? Use the Soil Triangle, **Fig. 9-1**.

   _____

4. How does your answer compare to the qualitative method?

   _____

5. Is your soil type consistent with your percolation test results from Part Six? How so?

   _____

   _____

   _____

6. Compare your soil texture to the results others in the class have measured. Which sites were the most sandy, silty, or claylike?

   _____

   _____

7. Hypothesize why the soils are the way they are. How were they formed?

   _____

   _____

   _____

   _____

8. Look for patterns in the class data. On separate paper, draw a map of the area and plot the soil types of the class.

9. If there were plants growing naturally in the area where you took your samples, do they prefer a particular soil type?

_____

_____

PART THREE: SOIL MOISTURE

You will now measure the amount of water in your soil sample. Make a small tray of aluminum foil and record the mass. Then put several spoonfuls of soil on the tray and again record its mass. Now put the tray with your sample into a drying oven for 24 hours, at a temperature of 90–95°. After heating the soil to dryness, let the sample cool and again record its mass. Any mass loss will most likely be water.

1. Determine the percent water, by mass, in your sample. Show your work.

   Mass of aluminum tray empty: _____ g

   Mass of tray + soil sample before heating: _____ g

   Mass of tray + soil sample after heating: _____ g

   Mass loss due to heating: _____ g _____ % mass loss

2. Compare the soil moisture of your sample to your soil texture results in Part Two.

_____

_____

_____

3. Is there a pattern or correlation between soil moisture and texture, based on results by other members of the class? Describe it.

_____

_____

_____

PART FOUR: PERCENT ORGANIC MATTER

To measure the organic matter, you will have to burn the soil at high temperature to convert as much of it as possible into CO_2 and H_2O. Since the general procedure involves measuring mass loss, you must first ensure the dryness of the sample.

Record the mass of a clean, dry porcelain crucible and fill it about ¾ full of your soil sample. Place it in the drying oven overnight at a temperature of 90–95° C to drive off the water. When that has been accomplished, record the mass of the soil and crucible.

In a fume hood, place the crucible on a ring stand, using an iron ring and pipe-stem triangle. Heat it gently for a few minutes and then heat it as hot as you can for about 30 minutes. Shut off the burner and allow the crucible to cool. Now record the mass of the crucible and soil again.

1. Calculate the organic matter in the sample (the loss of mass). Show your work.

   Mass of empty crucible: _____ g

   Mass of crucible + dry soil: _____ g

   Mass of crucible + soil after heating: _____ g

   Percent organics in sample: _____ %

2. Why is it not necessary to measure the mass of the soil alone?

   _____

   _____

3. Give at least three reasons why it is important to have organic material in soil.

   _____

   _____

PART FIVE: SOIL POROSITY

Porosity is the amount of air space in a soil sample. Porosity is important because it determines the ease with which water, oxygen, and nitrogen can work their way down to the root zones of plants. The creation of aquifers also depends on pore spaces between soil particles.

To determine the porosity of your soil, fill a 250-mL beaker to the 200 mL mark with dried soil and tamp down gently. Fill a 100-mL graduated cylinder to the 100 mL mark with water. Gently pour the water onto the surface of the soil until the soil is completely saturated and water just starts to pool up on the surface. Measure the amount of water left in the graduated cylinder. The amount used is the amount of pore space in your sample.

1. Calculate porosity as the percent of pore space compared to the volume of dry soil. Show your work.

   Volume of soil: _____ mL   Volume of water used: _____ mL

   Porosity: _____ %

The **dry percolation rate** is a measure of how fast water flows through dry soil. This measure is particularly important in the design of leaching fields for septic systems in areas without sewer systems. The excess fluids from the septic tank must disperse quickly over a wide area.

Preparation Place a small piece of filter paper in the neck of a 16-oz water bottle that has been cut off to act as a funnel. You will fill the funneled section with soil samples to 1 cm of the top. Set the funnel section into the remaining, bottom part of the water bottle so that it collects the water as it drains through the soil sample. Set up three of these apparatuses, one for a sample of sand, one for a sample of clay, and one for your soil sample.

Percolation rate is measured in cubic centimeters of water per surface area of sample per second. Calculate the cross-sectional area of the funnel and give this area in square centimeters, a value that should be the same for all three set-ups. Pour water onto the surface of each sample and record from the time the water hits the surface to the time a measurable amount of water collects on the bottom of the bottle. Measure the water volume and record the elapsed time.

1. Record your measurements in **Table 9-1**.

	Sand	Clay	Your Sample
Sample Area			
Time Elapsed			
Water Volume			

Table 9-1

2. Calculate the percolation rate for all three samples. Show your work including proper units.

3. Discuss the patterns in your values.

_____

_____

_____

In this test you will collect and count macroinvertebrates in your soil sample.

Preparation Cut the top off a 2-liter clear soda bottle 2 to 3 cm below where the sides become parallel. This will be the funnel to hold the soil sample. Pour about 20–25 mL of ethanol into the bottom part of the bottle and place the funnel section on top. Place a small section of wire mesh in the neck of the funnel, then fill with your soil and humus sample to about 2 cm from the rim.

Put the apparatus in a warm quiet place so it will not be disturbed. Set a heat lamp about 10 cm above the surface of the soil to speed the drying and help drive the organisms to the bottom of the funnel, where they will fall through the mesh into the ethanol to be identified and counted.

1. After five to six days, pour the ethanol sample into a petri dish. With proper ventilation, use a hand lens to identify, count, and draw the life forms that you have collected.

2. Explain what role these various organisms play in your soil.

_____

_____

_____

_____

_____

3. How do your soil populations compare with those of others in class? Describe any patterns.

_____

_____

_____

_____

_____

PART EIGHT: SOIL FERTILITY ANALYSIS

Four variables are important in determining the fertility of soils. They are: pH and the amounts of nitrogen, phosphorous, and potassium. The values of each of these components can serve as a limiting factor in the growth of plants.

1. Use soil test kits and/or CBL2s to determine the values of each variable for your sample.

   pH: _____   Nitrogen: _____

   Phosphorous: _____   Potassium: _____

2. Based on your results of these tests, which nutrients are low in your soil sample?

   _____

   _____

   _____

   _____

3. What is the ideal pH range for the plants that were growing where you collected your sample? Did the plants look healthy there? Compare their general appearance to your results.

   _____

   _____

   _____

   _____

FOLLOW-UP INVESTIGATION

From the lab you should have a reasonably complete analysis of your soil, and from your text and class an understanding of what soil characteristics are good for growing plants. Based on your analysis and using the soil in which you grew your first lettuce crop, now remediate your soil to make it better able to support a second lettuce crop. You may need to add more nutrient, balance the pH, adjust the soil texture, add organics, or take other measures.

Once the soil is remediated, add it to another cup and prepare it as you did the first. Plant more lettuce seeds, add water, and set aside in warm sunlight. For two weeks, take care of your crop, keep daily notes as before, and monitor the progress of your lettuce. Aim to have enough lettuce for a taste comparison test, if possible, with the first crop.

CONCLUSIONS

Prepare your lab report. It should contain the following:

1. This lab guide with all the information and questions filled in and complete.

2. Daily journals for your preliminary and final lettuce crops.

3. Summaries of your test results.

   a. Describe the vegetation growing in your soil when you collected it.

   b. What correlations did you find between soil fertility and the organisms you found in your sample?

   c. Give two examples of how the results on one test are related to other tests.

   d. Outline the composition of your original soil and what you did to correct the deficiencies.

   e. Explain the logic of your remediation procedure and the expected outcomes.

4. Discussion: How does the growth of lettuce after remediation compare with lettuce planted before you did these experiments? Compare growth rate, color, number of leaves, and survival rate of the two crop samples.

5. Discussion: Assuming you did the taste test with the lettuce grown in the remediated soil, tell how the lettuces of different students compared.

   a. How did they taste, compared to each other? (They should all be of the same variety of lettuce and from seeds from the same source.)

   b. What could account for the difference in the tastes?

INVESTIGATION

10

Soil Salinization:
An Experimental Design

PURPOSE

➤ Develop an experimental design to investigate how salinization affects germination of various species of crop seeds

➤ Determine at what salt concentrations seeds no longer germinate

BACKGROUND

Most of the fertile and easily farmed land in the world is either now under cultivation or is developed for other purposes. This leaves less desirable arid land that will need irrigation to be farmed to feed the Earth's growing population. Soils in dry regions are generally rich in nutrients because there is little water to leach them below the root zone. These regions can be made to grow crops only with irrigation. Much of this water is pumped from underground aquifers containing dissolved mineral salts. As the water is sprayed onto the crops, some of it evaporates because of the low humidity. Low concentrations of salt on the land are not a problem. But over time the salts collect on or near the soil surface, where they eventually interfere with the germination and growth of the crops by removing water from plant cells. The salts decrease the osmotic potential of the soil so plants cannot take up water.

Soil **salinization** is a problem wherever irrigation is used in arid areas. These include the central valley of California and other areas of the American west, the Middle East, central Siberia, and China. In some areas, the summer irrigation effects are attenuated by the winter snows, which wash the salts back down below the root level. In some parts of the world, such as Saskatchewan, Canada, the water table contains high concentrations of salt and is near the surface. In the summer, the heat causes the water to evaporate out, leaving high levels of salt in the soil. In the United States, soil salinity costs billions of dollars and has become a cost of doing business. In the developing world, it is a matter of life and death.

Many salt ions are involved in soil salinization, such as sodium, calcium, magnesium, potassium, carbonate, chloride, and sulfate. The most common, by far, are sodium and chloride. For convenience, your team will study the effects of NaCl, ordinary table salt. An assumption will be made that the effect of NaCl will be characteristic of all the salts on the germinating seeds. Recall that fresh water has a salinity of 0.5% or less. The concentration of salt in the ocean, near U.S. coasts, is about 3.5% by mass. For comparison, a saturated solution of NaCl at room temperature is about 36% salt by mass.

Problem

You and your partners will act as a team of consultants hired by a group of farmers who are concerned about how increasing salt concentrations in their soil will affect their crops. Design a controlled experiment to measure how increasing salt concentrations interfere with the germination of four different types of crop seed.

Materials

- NaCl
- 4 species of crop seeds
- petri dishes
- sealable plastic bags
- spreadsheet or other graphing software
- potting soil
- paper cups

Procedure

Step 1 Salt concentrations to test should include at least eight concentrations from 0% to 4%. Since some plants are very sensitive to salt, include concentrations of 0.01%, 0.1%, 0.5% and 1%.

Step 2 To allow for differences among the seeds, use at least 10 seeds in each test. You can also use potting soil in paper cups or petri dishes.

Step 3 It is recommended that you use petri dishes as test vessels, placing them in sealable plastic bags to cut down on water evaporation, which increases salinity over time.

CONCLUSIONS

Your team's final report to the farmers should contain:

1. Cover sheet with brief overview of your experimental design.

2. Procedures and equipment used.

3. Data tables.

4. Graphic presentation of experiment (it is recommended that you use a spreadsheet program such as Excel for the graphing).

5. Analysis of the graphs.

6a. Conclusions, based on your data, about what crops to grow under which conditions.

  b. Recommendations of crops, other than those tested, that might be more tolerant of high salinities. (This will involve additional research.)

7. The **Threshold Level of Toxicity** and **LD-50** for each seed type, indicated on your graphs.

8a. A plan to remediate the soils if the salt concentration reaches toxic levels.

  b. Recommendations for alternative irrigation methods tailored to the specific crops.

National *and* **Local Water Use**

PURPOSE

> Use the Internet to gather and interpret water use data at the national, state, and local levels

> Analyze water use patterns over time to compare consumption levels with local rainfall

Materials

• topographic and other maps of your local water supply area

INTRODUCTION

Worldwide, fresh water use is increasing. This trend is because the human population is growing and, as the world becomes more industrialized, humans' per capita use is also on the increase. A United Nations publication reports that global water use over the 20th century grew twice as fast as the human population. Water use in the United States also has increased faster than its population.

Fig. 11-1

Global Water Consumption By Type of Use

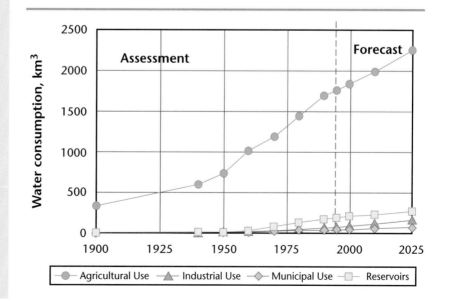

Water falls to Earth as precipitation, where it can either evaporate, run off the surface, or percolate down into the soil to become groundwater, as shown in the illustration of the **hydrologic cycle**. Our land-use decisions play a large role in where the water goes after it hits Earth. In urban areas nearly half of the water becomes runoff, mostly through storm sewers. This water usually cannot be used by humans as it makes its way back to the sea. But in undeveloped areas, at least 50% of the water recharges underground aquifers. As urban regions expand and become more populous, the amount of available water decreases.

Fig. 11-2

The Hydrologic Cycle

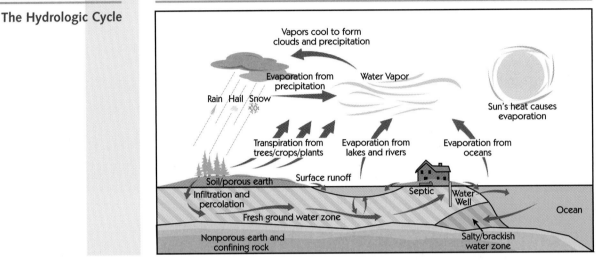

PART I: NATIONAL ANALYSIS

Access data from the following Web site:

http://wwwga.usgs.gov/edu/tables/dltotal.html

From the data table of "Total Water Use in the U.S.," calculate the per capita use of fresh water for each state. (*Take note of units*: Population is given in thousands and water use in millions of gallons.)

1. Per capita, what are the ten states that use the most water and the ten states that use the least water?

_____

_____

_____

_____

2. Look for patterns in the total water use of the states compared to their populations.

   a. Why do you think some of the states are such high water consumers?

   _____

   _____

   _____

Laboratory Investigations for AP Environmental Science

b. What industries account for such high levels of use?

_____

_____

c. Where do these high-use states rank in terms of total population?

_____

_____

3. Determine the location of states with lower per capita use.

    a. Why is their water use so much lower?

_____

_____

    b. How do these lower-use states rank in population size?

_____

_____

4. Look for patterns in your findings for Questions 2 and 3.

    a. What do the patterns tell about water use in differing parts of the country?

_____

_____

    b. What are three examples of conflicts that arise over competition for water?

_____

_____

5. Determine which states use more ground water than surface water.

    a. How do their aquifers get recharged?

_____

_____

    b. Does the recharge rate keep up with the rate of use?

_____

_____

    c. Give two potential reasons for aquifer resources being diminished, based on their geographic location and annual rainfall.

_____

_____

6. Find which states are in drier parts of the U.S.

    a. Which of these states use more surface water?

    _____

    _____

    b. How is such surface water use possible? Where does this water come from? How is it stored?

    _____

    _____

PART II: STATE ANALYSIS

In this part you will research how water use matches the water supply for your own state. You may search for reservoir or ground water levels on your state Web site or, as an alternative, access the United States Geologic Survey site and select your state there: http://water.usgs.gov/

1. Analyze how the water level has changed over time.

    a. What seasonal patterns do you observe, if any?

    _____

    _____

    b. If there are patterns in the water levels, why do they occur?

    _____

    _____

Your state university, Geologic Survey, Department of Environmental Protection or Division of Natural Resources has Web sites with rainfall data for your state or region.

2. Evaluate the average rainfall in your state, region, or city over the last 50 to 100 years.

    a. Is there an overall trend or has the pattern been somewhat random? Explain.

    _____

    _____

    b. How do the last five years fit into the pattern?

    _____

    _____

c. How do the data relate to the average temperature? Is there a relationship?

_____

_____

d. How do the patterns of El Niño and La Niña fit with these data?

_____

_____

PART III: LOCAL ANALYSIS

In this part of the project you will investigate where the water you consume comes from. If it is mostly surface water, it will most likely be collected in reservoirs. If you have well water, you will need to locate the recharge areas.

1. On topographic maps of your region, draw your watershed. If you have well water, draw in the region that feeds the recharge areas. Calculate the approximate area in square miles and then convert this to square feet ($1 \text{ mi}^2 = 2.79 \times 10^7 \text{ ft}^2$).

    a. You can approximate the amount of rainfall a watershed collects in a year by multiplying the surface area by the depth of the yearly rainfall total. (_Watch your units:_ Above, you calculated surface area in square feet.) Now calculate the volume of water collected, in cubic feet, by your watershed. Multiply the surface area by the yearly average rainfall.

    b. If 1 ft^3 of water equals 7.5 gal, how many gallons of water fall in your watershed in an average year?

2. Not all water from rainfall is stored where it can be used by people. Some evaporates directly or through the vegetation, and more is drawn off through storm sewers. The portion that percolates into the ground to be taken up through wells or that collects in reservoirs depends on what occupies the land. Local maps of your area may be helpful for the questions that follow.

    a. The average American uses about 100 gallons of water per day. Using population figures for your watershed, what is the daily water consumption in gallons?

b. What is the yearly consumption of water in your watershed?

c. For the sake of this exercise, assume that 50% of the annual rainfall is available for use. Does your watershed produce enough water to replace what is consumed? How great is the surplus or deficit?

_____

_____

3. Make an analysis of how the water gets to the reservoirs in your area and over what terrain the water passes.

a. Describe the land use in your watershed. Estimate how much of the land is covered by vegetation, wetlands, commercial and industrial areas, and housing.

_____

_____

_____

_____

b. As the water travels through the watershed, what are some of the threats to its safety based on land use?

_____

_____

_____

_____

4. How is your water treated for public use? How is it distributed?

_____

_____

_____

5. List and describe five ways communities can encourage water conservation.

_____

_____

_____

_____

_____

INVESTIGATION

12

Lab

Water Quality Index

PURPOSE

➤ Perform tests to determine the Water Quality Index (WQI) of a local body of water

➤ Perform follow-up WQI tests to establish an ongoing record and basis for possible water remediation

INTRODUCTION

The Water Quality Index (WQI) was developed in the early 1970s in an effort to compare the quality of water from all parts of the country. Over one hundred water-quality experts were called together to create this standard means of using one number to represent nine criteria for calculating the degree of water quality for a given body of water. The results are used to decide whether the water may be considered healthy, to monitor it over time, and to assess it relative it to any other body of water on Earth.

This investigation prepares you to perform all nine tests to determine the WQI for a body of water of your choosing. (If you cannot do all nine tests, a way of approximating the WQI will be explained in a later section of the lab.) Usually these tests are repeated several times to get a full picture of how an ecosystem may change over a period of time.

Below are outlined the bases for these tests and what the tests measure.

Dissolved Oxygen (DO) Oxygen is not very soluble in water. What little gets into solution is vital to aquatic life and water quality. Most oxygen dissolved in streams, rivers, and lakes gets there by contact with the atmosphere. In streams and rivers, water splashing over rocks and waterfalls traps oxygen in the water. Waves on rivers and lakes also increase the oxygen level in solution. Photosynthetic plants in the water also contribute a significant amount of oxygen to the water column.

This test measures the amount of oxygen that is dissolved in the water and is available to the aquatic life that lives there. If the DO levels are too low, fish can drown. A DO that is too low is often an indicator of possible water pollution. It also shows a potential for further pollution downstream because the ability of the stream to self-cleanse will be reduced.

pH Pure water contains an equal amount of H^+ and OH^- ions. Hydrogen ions are acidic and the OH^- ions are basic, or alkaline. pH measures the $-\log$ of the H^+ concentration. A pH of 7 is neutral; it is equally acidic and alkaline. pH values below 7 become more acidic and they approach zero as the hydrogen ions increasingly outnumber the OH^- ions. As the values climb above 7, the water is said to be basic. The water becomes more alkaline as the values approach 14 and the OH^- ions outnumber the H^+ ions.

Many aquatic life forms are very sensitive to acid levels in the water. Pollution tends to make water acidic. Most bodies of water have the highest biological diversity when the pH is near 7.

Temperature Change (ΔT) Water temperature is a very important parameter for a body of water. Most physical and biological processes are affected by the temperature. Most aquatic life requires an optimum temperature range to thrive and, like terrestrial life, finds survival difficult at extreme temperatures. Higher water temperatures lower the amount of dissolved oxygen for two reasons. First, all gases are less soluble in warmer water. Second, warmer water increases the metabolic rate of aquatic organisms, which increases the consumption of food and dissolved oxygen.

The increase of water temperatures is called **thermal pollution**, and it is a significant problem on some bodies of water. Most thermal pollution comes from the industrialization of rivers and waterways. Industries, especially large power plants, use large amounts of water to cool their machinery and equipment. Along smaller bodies of water, cutting trees takes away the shade and allows water temperatures to rise. Another cause, large-scale logging, increases soil erosion and water turbidity, which, in turn, raises the water temperature to the detriment of aquatic life.

Fecal Coliform Coliforms are a form of bacteria that are found in the intestines of warm-blooded animals; their presence in lakes, streams, and rivers is a sign of untreated sewage in the water. Fecal coliforms can get into the water from untreated human sewage or from farms and runoff from animal feed lots. While fecal coliforms themselves are not harmful to humans, their measures indicate the presence of harmful pathogens.

Biological Oxygen Demand (BOD) Aerobic bacteria in water eat organic matter and at the same time remove oxygen. When the organic material in dead aquatic plants is decomposed, it releases the nutrients nitrogen and phosphorus. These nutrients trigger more plant growth and more nutrients, which further lower oxygen levels. If there is too large an amount of organic material in the water, the oxygen levels can drop below what is necessary for other aquatic life forms.

The BOD test gives an approximation of the level of biodegradable waste there is in the water. This biodegradable waste can be leaves and grass clippings from human activities, animal waste and manure from food production, wood pulp from paper mills, or many other carbon-based wastes. Water with a high BOD usually has a high bacteria count as well.

Nitrates Nitrates are a crucial nutrient in aquatic environments for synthesis of amino acids and proteins, but serious problems can result from **eutrophication**, or excessive nutrient levels. Excess nitrates get into waterways as nonpoint source fertilizers and from defective septic and sewage treatment systems. Nitrates can also get into the water from natural processes related to the **Nitrogen Cycle**. Most excessive amounts of nitrates come from human-based activities such as runoff from fertilized land, animal wastes from feedlots, and treated municipal waste effluent. Nitrate pollution effects both surface and ground water. It has been implicated as the primary cause of the dead zones in the Gulf of Mexico, the Chesapeake Bay and Long Island Sound. Nitrates also get reduced to nitrites, which can be harmful to humans and fish.

Total Phosphates (PO_4 — P) Phosphates are another essential nutrient for aquatic plants, but only in very low concentrations. Excessive amounts of phosphorus build up easily, and small amounts can contaminate large volumes of water. Phosphorus gets into water from many sources, such as fertilizers, sewage and detergents. Phosphorus exists in water in both organic and inorganic forms. The many forms of phosphorus can be measured separately, but this test will measure the combined phosphorus concentration, giving a better total estimate.

Total Dissolved Solids (TDS) Solids can be found in water in two forms, dissolved or suspended. Dissolved substances will pass through any filter commonly used in a lab. Suspended solids will be stopped by a filter because they are larger than individual atoms, ions, and molecules. This test measures the many solids found dissolved in water, usually in the form of such ions as sodium (Na^+), magnesium (Mg^{2+}), calcium (Ca^{2+}), chloride (Cl^-), hydrogen carbonate (HCO_3^{2-}), and sulfate (SO_4^{2-}).

Solids soluble in water can also be organic, though they are usually salts. A steady concentration of dissolved minerals is necessary for aquatic life—both as essential nutrients and to maintain the osmotic balance with the cells of organisms. Changes in concentration can lead to a weakening of the organism or even death. High levels of TDS can affect water clarity and photosynthesis and lead to a decline in the quality and taste of drinking water. Some sources of dissolved solids are road salts in winter, urban runoff through storm sewers, farm chemicals, sewage treatment effluent, and factors that increase soil erosion such as road building and clear-cut logging.

Turbidity or Total Suspended Solids (TSS) This is a measure of how light is scattered in the water column due to solids that do not dissolve but are small enough to be suspended in the water. The higher the turbidity, the murkier the water. Turbidity keeps light from penetrating into the water and interferes with plant photosynthetic oxygen production and primary productivity. Darkened water holds more heat, increasing the water temperature which in turn lowers the DO. Suspended solids can clog fish gills and, in the case of silt and clay settling to the bottom, also smother larvae and fill in nesting sites. These solids may come from soil erosion or channelization from dredging. Increased water flow rates erode stream banks and allow the water to carry a heavier load of particles, storm and sanitary sewage effluent, and increased algae growth.

Calculating the WQI first requires the results of nine test measurements. These test values are then converted into Q-values by using graphs. The Q-values are multiplied by a weighting factor and then added up to determine the final WQI number that measures the overall water quality.

Materials

- thermometer
- water collecting bottles (clear)
- water collecting bottles (black)
- eye protection gear
- 0.1 M HCL
- 100-mL beaker

- 250-mL beaker
- long pole
- tape
- nonstretching rope or twine
- rubber gloves

Note: Several of the WQI test measurements may be obtained by two or more methods. Discuss with your teacher which of the methods is to be followed for each test, then obtain the procedures and any additional materials required.

Test Procedures

The following directions describe how to get the results of each test and locate its Q-factor. After the tests are performed and recorded you will find instructions for using a worksheet (see **Fig. 12-11**) to establish the WQI for your body of water.

Dissolved Oxygen Test

Temperature drastically affects the solubility of oxygen in water. To determine the Q-factor for DO you will have to find the **percent saturation** of oxygen for your sample. This can be done by finding the DO and water temperature and then using a nomograph to find the percent saturation.

There are three ways to determine the DO. The first is a traditional wet chemistry method called the Winkler Method. The second is a test kit with prepackaged chemicals, and the third an electronic device such as a CBL2 and DO sensor. Your teacher will select the method for this test and inform you of the procedure.

Step 1   Take the temperature of the water where you collect your sample. Hold the thermometer at the top so that your body will not affect the temperature. Lower the thermometer 10 cm (4 in.) into the water and wait for the temperature to stabilize. Record it on your lab sheet.

Step 2   When collecting your sample, it is important that you fill the collecting bottle to overflow and that there are no air bubbles when you cap the bottle.

Step 3   Once you determine the DO for your sample, find the percent saturation using the nomograph (**Fig. 12-1**).

   a. Put a pencil mark for your recorded temperature on the temperature scale and another mark for your DO reading on that scale.

   b. Now with a ruler connect the two marks with a straight line.

OXYGEN SATURATION CHART

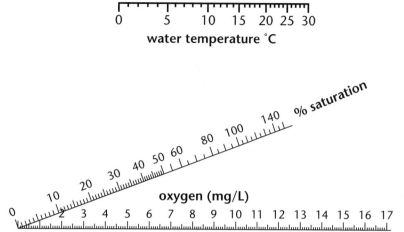

Fig. 12-1

c. The percent saturation can be read from the percent saturation scale where the line crosses the scale. Over 90% saturation is a sign of good water quality.

d. Record the percent saturation on your lab sheet.

Step 4 Now find the Q-value, using **Fig. 12-2**. Locate your percent saturation on the *x*-axis, follow vertically to the curved line on the graph, then read left, across to the *y*-axis.

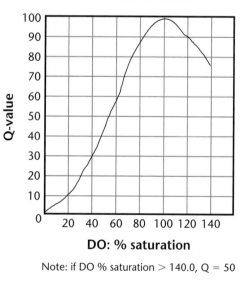

DO Test Results

Note: if DO % saturation > 140.0, Q = 50

Fig. 12-2

Step 5 Record your Q-value on the worksheet for calculating the WQI.

pH Test

As with DO, there are a number of ways to measure the pH of a water sample. Your teacher will give you directions for the method you will follow.

Step 1 Find the Q-value by using the graph. Find your pH measurement on the *x*-axis and read the Q-value for it on the *y*-axis.

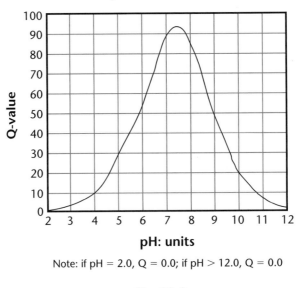

pH Test Results

Note: if pH = 2.0, Q = 0.0; if pH > 12.0, Q = 0.0

Fig. 12-3

Step 2 Record the Q-value on the worksheet for calculating the WQI.

Change in Temperature (ΔT) Test

To measure the temperature change of your body of water, you will have to record the temperature in two places, about 1 mile apart, using the same thermometer. (*Lab Hint:* It is easier to do this on a stream or river.) Choose conditions as similar as possible—same amount of shade, flow rate, and depth.

Step 1 Hold the thermometer near the top and insert it about 10 cm (4 in.) into the water.

Step 2 Wait for the temperature to stabilize.

Step 3 Go up or down stream, about one mile from your first test site, and record the temperature again.

Step 4 Record your temperatures, in °C, on your lab sheet.

Step 5 Subtract the temperatures and record that value on your lab sheet.

Step 6 Record the difference in temperature to find the Q-value from the graph (**Fig. 12-4**). Record the Q-value on the worksheet for calculating the WQI.

Laboratory Investigations for AP Environmental Science

Temperature Change Test Results

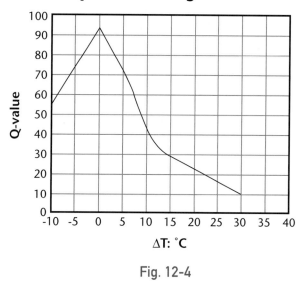

Fig. 12-4

Fecal Coliform Test

Not all schools will elect to do this section of the lab because of time, equipment and procedure constraints. Ask your teacher whether and how you are to perform this test.

Step 1 Be sure to wear goggles, mask, and rubber gloves.

Step 2 These test results are reported as number of colonies/100 mL of solution.

Step 3 Use the number of colonies on the *x*-axis of the graph to find the Q-value on the *y*-axis.

Step 4 Record your Q-value on the worksheet for calculating the WQI.

Fecal Coliform Test Results

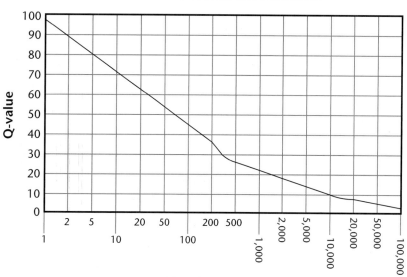

FC: colonies/100 mL

Note: if FC > 50^3, Q = 2.0

Fig. 12-5

You will need at least 2 sample bottles for dissolved oxygen, one clear and another black. Be sure that you do not trap any air bubbles in the bottles. The black bottle(s) can be painted black, wrapped in black electrical tape, or completely covered with aluminum foil.

Step 1   To sample the water, reach out as far from shore as you safely can. Collect your samples near the bottom of the body of water, where the BOD will probably be the highest. If you sample by hand, wear gloves. If the water is deep, tape the bottles to the end of a long pole to reach near the bottom.

Step 2   If you suspect the water to have a high BOD, collect 5 black bottle samples, rather than 1, and store them in the dark at 20° C or 68° F (see **Alternative Method** below).

Step 3   For the sample in the clear bottle, follow the procedures you used for the dissolved oxygen test and measure the DO.

Step 4   Place the black bottle in a dark, light-restricted place for 5 days at a temperature of 20° C (68° F). This is close enough to room temperature if you do not have an incubator.

Step 5   After 5 days, repeat the steps needed to measure the DO for the sample in the black bottle.

Step 6   Now determine the BOD by subtracting the DO of the black bottle after 5 days from the DO of the clear bottle measured on the first day.

Step 7   Find the BOD, in mg/L, on the *x*-axis of the graph and read the Q-value on the *y*-axis.

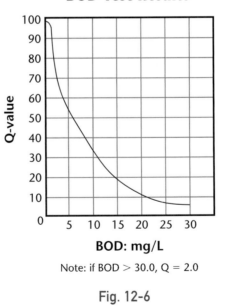

BOD Test Results

Note: if BOD > 30.0, Q = 2.0

Fig. 12-6

Step 8   Record the Q-value on the worksheet for calculating the WQI.

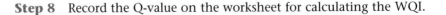

Alternative Method (In Case of High BOD)   If your body of water has a large amount of organic matter or sewage, the oxygen demand may be too high for the procedure above to indicate accurately.

a. One alternative method is to measure the DO initially and then every day for 5 days. If the DO falls below 4 mg/L, resaturate the remaining samples.

b. To resaturate a sample, pour the collected water into a clean, slightly larger bottle, with lid, and strongly shake for 1 minute. Uncap the bottle to let in air for about 1 minute, recap the bottle and again shake vigorously. Pour the water back into the original collection bottle and reseal without air bubbles for further testing.

Nitrate Test

There are several methods that can be used to measure the nitrate level. One method is to use a test kit and follow the directions to determine the nitrate concentration. Another method is to use an electronic sensor such as the Vernier Nitrate Ion Selective Electrode CBL2. Your teacher will have the directions for the method you will use.

Step 1   To measure the nitrate level, you will have to take your 100 mL sample at least 10 cm (4 in.) below the water surface and as far from shore as is safe. If you need to sample the water beyond arm's length, attach your collecting bottle to the end of a long pole and carefully reach the proper depth.

Step 2   Find the nitrate concentration, in mg/L, on the *x*-axis of the graph.

Step 3   Read up to the line and then find the Q-value on the *y*-axis.

Step 4   Record the Q-value on the worksheet for calculating the WQI.

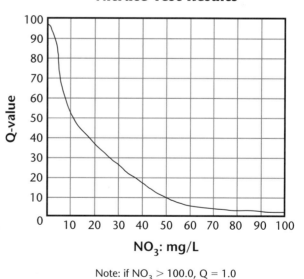

Nitrate Test Results

Note: if $NO_3 > 100.0$, Q = 1.0

Fig. 12-7

Total Phosphate Test

There are several methods to measure the total phosphate level. One method is to use a test kit and follow the directions to determine the phosphate concentration. Another method is to use an electronic sensor such as the Vernier Phosphate Colorimeter and CBL2. Your teacher will have directions for the method you use.

Step 1 It is important to use very clean glassware for this test. Phosphates can stick to glass and give an incorrect measurement. Soak all glassware in 0.1M HCl for at least one-half hour and then thoroughly rinse with distilled water. **BE CAREFUL:** HCl is very corrosive, painful on your skin and dangerous to your eyesight. **WEAR EYE PROTECTION.**

Step 2 To measure the total phosphate level in the water, you will have to take your 100 mL sample at least 10 cm (4 in.) below the surface and as far away from shore as is safe. If you need to sample the water beyond arm's length, attach your collecting bottle to the end of a long pole and carefully reach the proper depth.

Step 3 Find the total phosphate concentration, in mg/L, on the *x*-axis of the graph.

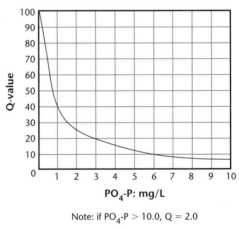

Total Phosphate Test Results

Note: if PO_4-P > 10.0, Q = 2.0

Fig. 12-8

Step 4 Read up to the line and then find the Q-value on the *y*-axis.

Step 5 Record the Q-value on the worksheet for calculating the WQI.

Total Dissolved Solids Test

There are two easy methods to measure the TDS of a water sample. The first method involves evaporating the water away and then recording the mass of the residue. The other is to measure the electrical conductivity of the unfiltered solution and convert the value to TDS. The Evaporation Method is outlined first.

Evaporation Method
Step 1 Heat a clean 250-mL beaker for 3–5 minutes to ensure that it is dry. Let it cool and then record its mass.

Step 2 Set up a funnel and filter in an iron ring on a ring stand.

Step 3 Filter enough of your water sample to collect 200 mL of solution.

Step 4 Carefully add 200 mL of the filtered sample to the clean dry beaker from Step 1 and place it on a hot plate to evaporate away all the water. (*Lab Hint:* If a Bunsen burner is the heat source, use a low flame and be careful not to let the water spatter, which will remove some solids and lead to a significant error.)

Step 5 After you are sure all the water has evaporated, allow the beaker and contents to cool, then record its mass in milligrams (mg).

Step 6 Subtract the mass of the empty beaker from Step 1 and record the change in mass. This is the mass of the TDS in 200 mL of sample.

Step 7 Multiply the mass of solids in your beaker by 5 to calculate the TDS in mg/L.

Step 8 Find the TDS on the *x*-axis of the graph.

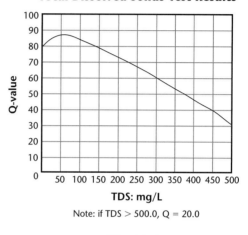

Total Dissolved Solids Test Results

Note: if TDS > 500.0, Q = 20.0

Fig. 12-9

Step 9 Read up to the line and then find the Q-value on the *y*-axis.

Step 10 Record the Q-value on the worksheet for calculating the WQI.

Electronic Method Your teacher will have detailed instructions if you are to use an electronic conductivity sensor, such as the Vernier Conductivity Sensor and the CBL2 or LabPro. After you get your reading from the sensor, use steps 8–10 above to find the Q-value.

Turbidity or Total Suspended Solids (TSS) Test

This test also can be done two ways. Your body of water and your teacher will determine which method to use. One method uses a Secchi Disk and the other electronic devices such as a spectrophotometer, colorimeter, or turbidity sensor calibrated to NTU's.

Secchi Disk Method The Secchi disk is a flat round plate 8 inches in diameter with pie slice-shaped quarters painted alternately white and black. A weight is suspended beneath it to let it sink when lowered in the water. The disk is attached to a thin nylon rope or chain with depth markings marked off in feet. (If you make your own disk, do not use cotton clothes line, which stretches. If you use a wire-centered cord, be sure it is not kinked and can be stretched out straight for measuring.)

Step 1 From a boat or dock, slowly lower the disk into the water horizontal to the surface.

Step 2 Keep lowering slowly until you cannot see any of the disk.

Step 3 Record the depth, in feet and inches, at which the disk disappears.

Step 4 On the graph, find the depth on the *x*-axis.

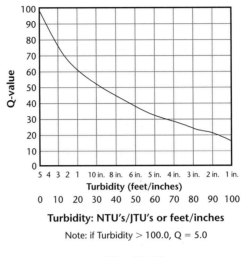

Total Suspended Solids Test Results

Turbidity: NTU's/JTU's or feet/inches

Note: if Turbidity > 100.0, Q = 5.0

Fig. 12-10

Step 5 Read up to the line and then find the Q-value on the *y*-axis.

Step 6 Record the Q-value on the worksheet for calculating the WQI.

Electronic Method Your teacher will give you instructions on how to use the electronic sensor. It will probably measure in NTU's.

Step 1 On the graph, find the NTU on the *x*-axis.

Step 2 Read up to the line and then find the Q-value on the *y*-axis.

Step 3 Record the Q-value on the worksheet for calculating the WQI.

CALCULATE THE WATER QUALITY INDEX (WQI)

Step 1 Be sure you have recorded all of your test results and Q-values on the worksheet (**Fig. 12-11**).

Step 2 For each test, multiply the Q-value by the weighting factor and place the product in the TOTAL column.

Step 3 Add the totals of all nine tests and record the sum at the bottom. This is the WQI for your body of water.

Fig. 12-11

WQI Worksheet

Test	Test Results	Q-Value	Weighting Factor	TOTAL
Dissolved Oxygen	% Sat		0.17	
pH	units		0.11	
Temperature Change	°C		0.10	
Fecal Coliform	colonies/100mL		0.16	
BOD	mg/L		0.11	
Nitrate	mg/L		0.10	
Total Phosphates	mg/L		0.10	
Total Dissolved Solids	mg/L		0.07	
Total Suspended Solids	feet or NTU's		0.08	

WQI = __________

Step 4   If you did not do all nine tests, you can approximate the WQI by using the results for those tests that you did perform.

Step 5   Add the totals for those tests performed. Record your result here:

_____

Step 6   Add the weighting factors for the tests performed. Record the sum here:

_____

Step 7   Divide the Step 5 value by the Step 6 value. Record the quotient here:

_____

Step 8   The Step 7 value is your estimated value for the WQI.

Step 9   You are now also able to rate the relative quality of your water samples. Use the chart below:

WQI Value	Water Quality Rating
91–100	Excellent Water Quality
71–90	Good Water Quality
51–70	Average Water Quality
26–50	Fair Water Quality
0–25	Poor Water Quality

Fig. 12-12

Follow-Up Procedures

1. Measure the WQI of the same body of water again after a few months. Keep a permanent record so the quality can be monitored over extended periods of time by other classes in the years to come.

2. If there are changes over time, try to determine the cause, then propose solutions to correct the problem and possible ways to remediate the water.

INVESTIGATION

13

Water Loss
Drop *by* Drop

PURPOSE

➤ Estimate household water loss from common leaks

➤ Extrapolate water loss to the surrounding community

INTRODUCTION

Leaks in water lines waste an extremely valuable and diminishing resource. New York City's Department of Environmental Protection estimates that leaks make up about 10% of the water demand of the city. In the last 15 years New York City has examined 31 million feet (5,871 mi) of the 33.6 million feet (6,364 mi) of water mains and eliminated 89 million gallons/day in leaks. The Boston Water and Sewer Commission surveyed 819 miles of its 1,182 miles of water distribution mains and fixed 427 leaks out of 444 leaks found, saving 7.16 million gallons/day.

Water losses in the developing world are more severe. In Iran in 1997, for example, 30% of the 3.8 billion cubic meters (1 trillion gallons) of treated water for the public was lost. This loss took place in a desert country with a population growing at an annual rate of 1.75%.

It might seem that with such large-scale losses in distribution systems, little domestic leaks are of little consequence. This exercise will show that when minor events occur often and long enough they result in large effects.

Problem

Determine the number of people living in your community or county. Assume the average household size is four people and there are approximately five water sources (faucets and toilets) in each household. Assume that two of the faucets leak at the rate of 1 drop/sec.

Analysis
Problems
Exercises
Questions

1. Calculate the volume of water lost by each household annually. Here are some useful equivalences. Explain any other assumptions you make.

20 drops = 1 milliliter   3.78 liters = 1 gal   1 gal = 0.133 ft³

2a. What is the total water loss in your community or county?

b. What percent of the total water consumption does that community loss represent? Assume a typical person uses 95 gal of water per day, on average.

3. Make an analogy to illustrate how much such a water loss really amounts to. The analogy should be an indication of the total volume.

_____

_____

_____

_____

4. Describe 10 actions you could take in your own home to conserve water. Estimate what percent of your total household consumption your savings represent.

_____

_____

_____

_____

_____

INVESTIGATION

14

Project

Water Diversions

PURPOSE

➢ Research the Internet and other sources to analyze the effects of water diversions on surrounding ecosystems and human communities

➢ Compare and contrast the problems and successes of various water diversions and describe possible remediations

INTRODUCTION

Humans have been diverting water for irrigation, flood control, and a constant drinking supply for thousands of years. When populations were small, the diversions were small. Over the last 150 years human populations have grown rapidly and our technical abilities have vastly improved. These two changes, worldwide, have led to many large-scale projects that have altered the environment of sizable regions. This investigation focuses on three major water diversions: the Salton Sea, Aral Sea, and the Colorado River.

Materials

- world atlas
- encyclopedia
- Internet access

1. Describe the location of the Salton Sea. What is the climate and geography of the area?

_____

_____

2. How did the Salton Sea form? Explain what role humans played.

_____

_____

_____

3. What is the present condition of this body of water? How has it changed over the last 25 years? Why?

_____

_____

_____

4. Describe several ways the Salton Sea has altered the ecosystem of the region. Explain the stability of that ecosystem. How is it changing over time?

_____

_____

_____

5. Outline three environmental and three economic reasons the Salton Sea is important.

_____

_____

_____

_____

_____

Questions

Exercises **Problems** **Analysis**

6. What steps are being taken to remediate the Salton Sea? What are the chances of success? Explain.

_____

_____

_____

_____

_____

7. Compare the similarities and differences between the Salton Sea and Lake Chad in sub-Saharan Africa.

_____

_____

_____

_____

_____

PART II: The Aral Sea

1. Find the location and other geographic information about the Aral Sea from a current atlas.

   a. Which former Soviet republics border the Aral Sea?

_____

_____

   b. Which rivers mainly supply the Aral Sea?

_____

_____

2. What government agency is responsible for the Aral Sea and its plight?

_____

_____

3. Why was the water supply to the Sea diverted?

_____

_____

_____

4. What resources did the Aral Sea supply to the local inhabitants?

_____

_____

5. Describe three negative environmental effects of the fading of this sea.

_____

_____

_____

_____

_____

6. Describe three economic impacts in the region because of the water diversion.

_____

_____

_____

7. How is the situation of the Salton Sea similar to the Aral Sea? How is it different?

_____

_____

_____

_____

_____

8. How would you describe this region today, other than as a "sea"?

_____

_____

_____

9. Explain five health effects on people related to the vanishing Aral Sea.

_____

_____

_____

_____

_____

_____

_____

_____

10. How can the Aral Sea be realistically rehabilitated?

_____

_____

_____

_____

11. Compare the situation in Mono Lake in California with that of the Aral Sea.

    a. How did the Mono Lake problem arise?

_____

_____

_____

_____

    b. Describe three ways the problems of Mono Lake are similar to those of the Aral Sea.

_____

_____

_____

_____

    c. Outline three ways the problems of Mono Lake differ.

_____

_____

_____

_____

_____

    d. Summarize the proposals and actions to remediate Mono Lake.

_____

_____

_____

_____

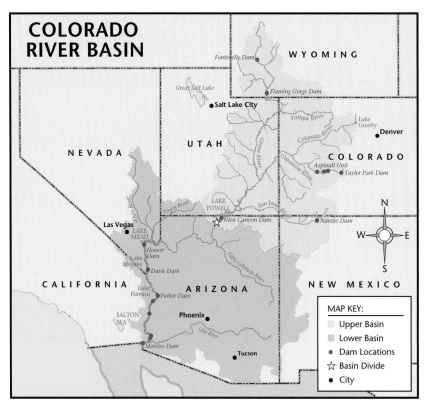

COLORADO
RIVER BASIN

Fig. 14-1: The Colorado flows across five states and parts of Mexico.

PART III: The Colorado River

1. Compare water diversion influences on the Colorado River with those on the Salton Sea and the Aral Sea. Describe three ways they are different.

2. Look at **Fig. 14-1**. Where is the source of the Colorado River? What are some of the main tributaries and their sources? What is the most important origin of the water in the Colorado River?

Laboratory Investigations for AP Environmental Science

3. Who decides where the water in the river system goes? How is the resource divided between the various states in the watershed and beyond?

_____

_____

_____

_____

4. How do the individual states use the water? Who are the top five consumers of the water?

_____

_____

_____

_____

5. Describe some of the conflicts that arise over water use. How are they usually resolved?

_____

_____

_____

_____

6. How are conflicts between public and private use managed?

_____

_____

_____

_____

7. Serious differences with Mexico exist concerning the amount of water the Mexicans receive from the river. Explain why this problem exists and what can be done to work out this dispute between the countries.

_____

_____

_____

_____

_____

_____

Questions

Analysis Problems Exercises

8. The Tigris and Euphrates Rivers cross international boundaries in their path to the Persian Gulf. Why is this problem potentially greater than the one that exists on the Colorado River?

_____

_____

_____

_____

9. Compare the problem of water diversions on the Yangtze River in China with those of the Colorado River.

_____

_____

_____

_____

10. The Three Gorges Dam on the Yangtze River is very controversial.

   a. Why is this dam being built?

   _____

   _____

   _____

   _____

   b. Describe how this dam differs from dams on the Colorado River, such as the Glen Canyon Dam or Hoover Dam, with respect to:

   • the disruption of human life
   • impact on the environment
   • archaeology
   • local culture and natural beauty

   _____

   _____

   _____

   _____

   _____

   _____

   _____

   _____

Net Primary Productivity

PURPOSE

➤ Measure net primary productivity (NPP) of rye grass, comparing NPP measurement methods for reliability

➤ Apply the NPP concept to problems of crop growth and higher trophic level support

INTRODUCTION

Net primary productivity (NPP) is defined as the amount of carbon from the atmosphere that gets added to green plants per unit of time. It is a rate, the quantity of new vegetable matter added per day, per week or per year. Net primary productivity is calculated as the total gain of biomass from photosynthesis minus the losses due to plant respiration. It is this net gain that is available to other organisms as food. The higher the NPP is in a region, the higher the overall biomass and diversity.

You will measure NPP by comparing the changes in dry mass of rye grass growth over the course of one week. The class will be divided into two groups. One group will follow the entire plant removal method and the other group will carry out the clipped grass procedure. Both procedures measure the net primary productivity as an increase in dry weight over a one week period.

Materials

- potting soil
- rye grass seeds
- aluminum foil
- plastic trays about 30 cm × 50 cm × 5 cm deep

1. Fill the trays with potting soil to near the top.

2. Plant rye grass seeds so that the seeds are no more than 0.5 cm apart.

3. Cover the seeds with a thin layer of the potting soil.

4. Water the trays enough to ensure that the soil is saturated but with no standing water.

5. Place the trays to expose them to sunlight or under artificial lights designed for plants.

6. Continue to water the seeds when necessary as they sprout and grow to grass plants.

7. It will take about two to three weeks for the plants to be large enough to start the experiment.

Procedures

Note: If you are experimenting in a classroom, space will be a consideration. Your group will not be able to harvest all the grass in a 1-m^2 plot. Your raw data will be added grams of carbon from a few plants over a few days. You will need to convert these data into units of grams of carbon per square meter per year (or g C/m^2/yr).

Entire Plant Removal Method (EPR)

Step 1   Take five complete plants, roots and all, from the soil, removing as much soil as possible.

Step 2   Place the plants on an open container made from aluminum foil, and put in the drying oven for 48 hours at a temperature between 90° C and 95° C.

Step 3   In the section of the tray from which you took your samples, count the number of plants in a 5 cm-by-5 cm area. Record this count in your data table.

Step 4   After the plants are dry, weigh and record the mass. This is the starting dry mass.

Step 5   Allow the remaining grass to grow for one week more, watering when necessary.

Step 6   Remove five more plants and repeat the drying and weighing procedure. This is the final dry mass.

Step 7   Find the difference in dry mass. This number is in grams of added carbon per five plants. Scale this value up by using the number of plants growing in 25 cm^2. Then convert units of cm^2 to m^2 and also the number of days between samples into years.

Step 8   Calculate and report the net primary productivity in units of grams of carbon per square meter per year.

Clipped Grass Procedure

Step 1 Harvest 15 plants, all from the same area in the tray, by cutting the plants 0.5 cm above the soil.

Step 2 In the section of the tray from which you took your samples, count the number of plants in a 5 cm-by-5 cm area. Record this count in your data table.

Step 3 Place the clippings on an open container made from aluminum foil, and put in the drying oven for 48 hours at a temperature between 90° C and 95° C.

Step 4 After the plants are dry, weigh and record the mass. This is the starting dry mass.

Step 5 Allow the remaining grass in the tray to grow for one more week.

Step 6 Harvest an additional 15 grass plants by clipping the plants 0.5 cm above the soil. Repeat the drying and weighing procedure. This is the final dry mass.

Step 7 Find the difference in dry mass. This number is in grams of carbon per 15 plants. Scale this value up by using the number of plants growing in 25 cm². Then convert units of cm² to m² and also the number of days between samples into years.

Step 8 Calculate and report the net primary productivity in units of grams of carbon per square meter per year`.

1. What is the definition of net primary productivity? Why is this rate such an important piece of information for ecologists?

_____

_____

_____

_____

_____

2. Compare the NPP figures from the entire plant method to those of the clip method. Explain why the figures are the way they are. Are they as you would expect? Why?

_____

_____

_____

_____

_____

_____

3. Which procedure appears to give the most reliable data? Why? How could you find a valid way to compare data from the two methods?

_____

_____

_____

_____

_____

4. Why are the results expressed as "net productivity" instead of "gross productivity"?

_____

_____

_____

_____

5. Grass seed could have been replanted on the plot from which the grass was removed in the EPR experiment and the amount of new plant growth compared and recorded as productivity. Comment on the reliability of such data.

_____

_____

_____

_____

6. Suppose the rye grass plants continued to grow at the same rate over a six-month growing season. What would be the net productivity for a field that is 1 km^2?

_____

_____

_____

_____

7. Comment on the availability of energy from the plant, if it is consumed by herbivores after the six-month growing season. Explain how energy availability affects the timing of farmers' harvest of their grain crops.

_____

_____

_____

_____

8. In the eastern United States, in particular from Massachusetts to Virginia, climax hardwood forests are being rapidly replaced with large, single-family homes and townhouse complexes. Based on the outcome of this investigation, explain one reason why the deer herds in those states have drastically increased.

_____

_____

_____

_____

9a. Design an experiment by which you could measure the net primary productivity of a field in the wild. Describe it.

b. How could this NPP be used to determine the number of herbivores that could be supported by the field? For example, how many cows could feed there?

c. How would you estimate the number of trophic levels that could be sustained in the field?

d. Describe how remote sensing could be used to determine the NPP of an area.

Eating *at a* Lower Trophic Level

Quantitative

PURPOSE

➤ Calculate and compare human food needs at different trophic levels, using the data to construct a biomass pyramid

➤ Analyze the benefits and drawbacks of eating at lower trophic levels on a global scale

BACKGROUND

A **trophic level**, or feeding level, is made up of all the organisms whose energy source is the same number of consumption steps from the sun in a given ecosystem. The trophic level of plants or producers is 1, while that of herbivores is 2 and that of animals that eat herbivores 3. Higher trophic levels can exist for animals even higher on the food chain. In this exercise you will compute numerical values for human energy needs based on diets at different trophic levels.

Problem

The owner of a soybean farm raises guinea hens for food and insect control. Guinea hens will eat grasshoppers and other insect pests and ticks. They also act as a "watchdog" by making a lot of noise when intruders approach their territory. The farmer allows the hens free range in his fields during the day and provides roosts for them at night.

For purposes of the following exercises, you may make these assumptions:

- the farmer lives on 1 hen/day for a year
- 1 hen eats 25 grasshoppers/day
- 1,000 grasshoppers have a mass of 1 kg
- 1 grasshopper requires about 30 g of soy/yr
- 1 human requires about 600 grasshoppers/day
- dry soybeans have about 3.3 cal/g

➤ Show all your math using *proper* units.

1. Calculate the number of grasshoppers a hen needs per year.

2. How many grasshoppers are needed for a year's supply of hens for the farmer each year?

3. What is the total mass, in kilograms, of the grasshoppers needed to feed all the hens for one year?

4. How many kilograms of soybeans are needed to feed all the grasshoppers for one year?

5. Estimates of early Native American hunter-gather societies indicate that a person could collect about 90 kg (200 lb) of grasshoppers per hour, when they are abundant. Now suppose the farmer chose to eat grasshoppers instead of hens. How many people could the grasshoppers feed, compared to the one person that the hen fed?

6. The farmer needs to consume 3,000 cal/day. If he ate only soybeans instead of the hens or the grasshoppers, how many people would his soybean crop feed (see your response to Question 4)?

7. Draw a **Biomass Pyramid**, using the data you have developed to this point. Why do most food chains not have a fourth and/or fifth trophic level?

8. Should people generally eat at a lower trophic level? It seems, by a simple analysis, that the Earth could support many more people if we all ate at a lower trophic level.

a. Outline three pros and three cons of such a practice.

_____

_____

_____

_____

_____

b. On average, cows produce 19 kilograms of protein/acre/year and soy produces 200 kilograms of protein/acre/year. Relate these data to the fact that people in the less-developed countries usually eat at lower trophic levels than those in developed countries.

_____

_____

_____

_____

9. Comment on the success of omnivores, such as coyotes, rats, and humans, and the fact that they can eat at many trophic levels.

_____

_____

_____

_____

_____

Exercises

Analysis

Problems

Exercises

10. List the foods you have eaten over the last five days.

_____

_____

_____

  a. Identify what trophic level each food came from.

_____

_____

_____

  b. Estimate what percent of the mass of the food in your diet comes from the first and second trophic levels.

_____

_____

  c. What percent of your diet comes from higher trophic levels?

_____

_____

_____

11. Large predatory fish, which may be part of your diet at times, usually exist at the third or fourth trophic level. Explain why it may not be a good idea to eat these fish often, if at all.

_____

_____

_____

_____

_____

_____

_____

_____

INVESTIGATION

17

Lab

Predator-Prey Simulation

PURPOSE

➤ Simulate and analyze the interactions between a predator population of coyotes and a prey population of mice

➤ Organize and graph data from the simulation, predicting future populations over several generations

➤ Compare simulation results to data taken from nature, and apply revised simulation techniques to other population problems

INTRODUCTION

Predator-prey interactions in a population are usually a feedback system. The prey population has a positive effect on the predator numbers, but the predator population has a negative effect on the prey numbers. The predator-prey relationship can be represented as changing cyclically with a phase diagram, as shown in **Fig. 17-1**.

Fig. 17-1

Generalized Scheme of Predator-Prey Relationship in Cyclical Change Through Time

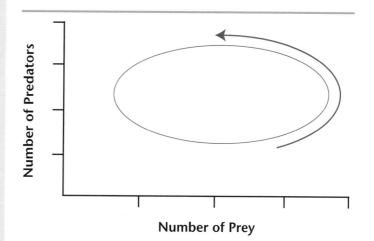

In the lower right quadrant, as the predator population rises, the prey population also rises. But as the predator numbers reach a particular value, the prey population starts to decrease, followed eventually by a decrease in the predator population as well (upper left quadrant). In time the predator population becomes small enough for the prey numbers to rebound and the process continues into another cycle. In nature the cycles are more complex than is indicated in the diagram, as there are many more influences on populations in the wild. In this investigation the factors will be confined simply to predator-prey numerical pressures.

Materials

- masking tape
- graphing paper
- construction paper
- Internet access
- spreadsheet and/or graphing software

Optional:

- computer simulations of predator-prey system

Procedure

Each lab group will need to set its own parameters for the simulation, as follows:

- how many mice are in the field under initial conditions
- the minimum number of mice a coyote needs to eat to survive and reproduce
- OPTIONAL: how many mice a coyote needs to eat *above the minimum* to produce 2 or more pups for the next generation

To generate data for the simulation, you will drop different-sized pieces of paper, representing mice and coyotes, onto a square marked out on the floor in the classroom. These pieces can be cut from sheets of graph paper to ensure size consistency.

Remember, the relationship between predator and prey is usually cyclical, and their corresponding numbers will rise and fall in some pattern. You will probably need at least 15 iterations of the simulation to see if you have a pattern. It may take some trial and error to determine the proper "rules" for your simulation to demonstrate a pattern. It is very possible that your model may produce chaotic variation. If this occurs, revamp your rules and continue.

Step 1 Using masking tape, mark off a "field" on the floor that is 50 cm (about 20 in.) square. If approved by your teacher, some groups should try smaller squares. Larger-sized "fields" will take too many coyotes and mice to be practical in the time allotted for this lab. (*Hint:* If your floor has tiles, use a certain number of them to delineate your field.)

Step 2 Write down all your group parameters and rules, including those for possible larger litters of pups.

_____

_____

_____

_____

_____

Step 3 Cut out pieces of paper to represent coyotes and mice. You will need many more mice than coyotes, probably about 300 mice to 15 coyotes. The actual number of each may vary based on the parameters you choose.

The pieces of paper should be of two sizes, possibly at a ratio of about 2:1, to simulate the feeding needs of the coyote. They can be squares cut from graph paper for uniformity or, if you are artistically inclined, silhouettes of the animals. Different groups may want to experiment with different size ratios and then compare their results at the end of the simulation.

Step 4 Drop the papers representing the starting number of mice into the square. They should fall randomly inside the borders of the "field." Experimentation will determine from how high the papers need be dropped to give consistent random falls within the square.

Step 5 Once your mice are distributed, drop 1 preying coyote into the field. For the coyote to survive and reproduce, it must fall directly on the number of mice determined by your parameters (see Step 2). Take the "eaten" mice out of the square. Assume that the remaining mice get to reproduce by doubling their number. This ends one generation.

Step 6 The next generation is represented by the new number of mice and they are preyed on by the number of surviving coyotes. If no coyotes survive a generation, start again with one coyote. If all the mice are eaten, start again with the same number as in the first round.

Step 7 Record the number of surviving mice and coyotes after each round in your Table of Data (**Fig. 17-2**).

Note: To monitor whether the relationship is going as expected, data can be entered directly into a spreadsheet or a graphing program as the simulation proceeds.

• If you enter the data into a spreadsheet such as _Excel_, when you are ready to make a graph, highlight your data and click on the chart icon. On the chart Wizard, select "Custom Types" and then scroll down to "Lines on Two Axes."

• You can also use graphing programs such as _Graphical Analysis_ to monitor the data after each generation. It is possible to use graphing calculators as well, but you will need a GraphLink cable to get the data and graph into a computer so that you can write up the lab.

Step 8 It is likely that the initial coyote did not land on the required number of mice needed to survive. If so, again drop a coyote on the square to represent a new animal migrating into the area looking to take advantage of a resource.

Step 9 Record your data for the second generation, based on the number of surviving mice and coyotes. Once more, if the coyote does not land on the required number of mice, start generation 3 with one coyote.

Step 10 Double the surviving mice and repeat. If the coyote lands on the necessary number of mice, it reproduces and yields one or more offspring for the next generation.

Step 11 Repeat this process for at least 15 iterations to see if you have a predictable pattern developing. If your data seem chaotic, rethink your conditions, make parameter adjustments here, and continue.

_____

_____

_____

_____

_____

_____

_____

_____

Step 12 As the coyote numbers increase, remove the mice eaten by each coyote in that generation. (As one coyote eats mice it is harder for the following animals to hunt successfully. In this way the simulation also models the effectiveness of superior hunters and nature's weeding out the less efficient.) Record the total population of each at the end of the generation.

Step 13 When your model seems to be producing a cyclical pattern, complete 25 iterations and graph the data.

Fig. 17-2

Data Table for
Predator-Prey Model

Generation Number	Mice (starting number)	Coyotes (starting number)
1		
2		
3		
4		
5		
6		
7		
8		
9		
10		
11		
12		
13		
14		
15		
16		
17		
18		
19		
20		
21		
22		
23		
24		
25		

Analysis

On a separate sheet of paper, place the data for both the mice and coyotes on the same graph so that the interrelationship can be easily observed. Use two y-axes, one on the left end of the x-axis and the other on the right end. The left one is for plotting the mice and the right one is for plotting the coyotes. Label each vertical axis separately. Label the x-axis "Time in Generations." Use one color line for the mice and another color for the coyotes.

1. What do you predict would happen to your results if your system was disturbed by some unforeseen, outside forces? To answer parts **a** and **b**, first draw the last cycle of your experimental graph free-hand. Continue graphing for at least three additional cycles to display your prediction.

   a. Draw on your graph and explain here what would happen if some coyotes died of disease or were driven off by larger predators or hit by cars.

   _____

   _____

   b. Draw on your graph and explain what would happen to the prey populations in the event of a fire, or of additional predators of another species moving in.

   _____

   _____

   c. How would it matter at what point in your simulation such disturbances occurred?

   _____

   _____

2. Search the Internet to find how your simulation compares to data of predator-prey systems taken from nature, such as those of owls and mice, lynx and snowshoe hare in Maine, or the moose-wolf system on Isle Royal in Michigan.

   a. Look for what general pattern exists for the data from nature.

   • How does the predator population vary when the prey numbers change?

   _____

   _____

   • Are the populations in phase with each other?

   _____

   _____

   • Are the population curves similar in shape? How do the curves differ from each other?

   _____

   _____

   b. Describe how your simulation data are similar or different. If your results are very different, explain why.

   _____

   _____

c. What could you do to adjust your "rules" (model) to better fit the natural patterns?

_____

_____

3. Compare your graphed data to the data of other groups in class.

    a. Which parameters generally made the most difference?

_____

_____

_____

    b. How could the initial parameters be changed to better simulate a natural system?

_____

_____

    c. If adjustments were made to a model in the middle of the simulation, how did the data then compare to the graphs of natural data?

_____

_____

4. How would the graphs look different if the predator were cold-blooded? How could information on such differences be used in examining the fossil record of dinosaurs to determine if a species was warm- or cold-blooded?

_____

_____

_____

5. Design a predator-prey population experiment using a planktonic rotifer, such as _Brachinus calyciflorus_, as the predator and the single-celled green algae, such as _Chlorella vulgaris_, as the prey. Predict what would happen to the populations if:

    a. a nutrient like nitrogen were added to the water. Explain why.

_____

_____

_____

    b. the nitrogen levels were reduced. Explain why.

_____

_____

6. How could this predator-prey method be used to model the spread of a disease, such as measles, SARS, ebola, or the flu, in a large population center?

_____

_____

_____

7. Describe at least three predator adaptations that make hunting easier. Articulate three adaptations of prey that help them escape predation.

_____

_____

_____

_____

_____

_____

_____

8. Are parasites predators? Explain.

_____

_____

_____

9. In this investigation you examined only the simple relation between changing prey populations and the number of predators. What other variables affect the number of predators and prey in a population? Describe four other possible factors.

_____

_____

_____

_____

10. Describe an example of a predator being used to control a prey population that is considered a pest. Explain scientifically why you believe this is a good idea or not.

_____

_____

_____

Extension

There are several computer simulations of various predator-prey systems. Find one and play it. Describe how the results of your model simulate results from computer models.

Shannon-Weiner Diversity Index

PURPOSE

➤ Collect and count organisms and species in several habitats

➤ Analyze and apply data to biodiversity problems using the Shannon-Weiner Diversity Index

BACKGROUND

A central theme in ecology is **biodiversity**, which often serves as a measure of the overall health of an ecosystem. Declining biodiversity can indicate that the ecosystem is undergoing some type of environmental stress. Further study can then help to pinpoint that stress.

There are many methods that ecologists use to calculate species diversity. The Shannon-Weiner Diversity Index is a common way of showing that diversity involves not only numbers of different species, but also how well each of these species is represented in different "habitats." The Shannon-Weiner value "H" can range from no diversity at 0.0 to a maximum diversity at 4.0. These values have no real meaning by themselves, but can be used to compare two communities or the same community at different times. The index was based on information theory developed some time ago by communication engineers. A large value of H indicates that if you randomly pick two organisms in your test area, the odds are the second individual will be different from the first. In this field investigation, your group will collect data and make calculations from the data. If you are unable to go outdoors to collect data as directed, ask your teacher for alternatives.

Materials

- index cards
- honey or other sweet bait
- tuna or cat food
- sealable bags
- hand lens
- table of natural logarithms

*Optional (see **Extension**):*

- plywood
- saw

Procedure

Step 1   Place the names of the students in your group on the bottom of ten 6 × 9-in. index cards.

Step 2   Bait five index cards by smearing the named side with something sweet like honey. Bait the other five cards with tuna or cat food. Divide the cards into 5 pairs of the two bait types.

Step 3   Place the pairs of cards near each other, bait side down, in five different locations (in the grass, near trees or a building foundation, etc.). Pin the cards as close to the ground as possible to attract organisms to the food and prevent them from blowing away.

Step 4   Number each site for identification purposes. Draw a map of the area that includes your sites and label the map with the ID numbers.

Step 5   Make a table of data to record the biotic and abiotic conditions. Approximate the moisture level or wetness of your areas and determine the temperature of each site. Also record any other differences in the habitats, biotic or abiotic, that you can measure or describe and that may aid in your analysis at the end of the experiment.

Step 6   Leave the cards in place for at least 24 hours.

Step 7   Collect the cards by carefully slipping each into its own zip-lock or other air-sealed bag with the proper ID number on it. The bags can then be placed in the refrigerator or freezer until you are ready to make your counts.

Step 8   For each card, count the number of organism types, and the number of individuals of each type, and record them on your data table. It is not necessary to identify the organisms to the species level, but you must agree among yourselves on what different types there appear to be. A hand lens will help in making distinctions.

Calculations

The most common equation for the Shannon-Weiner Index is:

$$H = -\text{sum } (p_i \ln p_i)$$

where H = Shannon-Weiner Diversity Index
                p_i = the ratio of the number of organisms of a species
                    to the total number of organisms
     $\ln p_i$ = the natural log of p_i

For each index card you used, complete a copy of the chart in **Fig. 18-1** to calculate an Index value.

Fig. 18-1

Index Calculation Chart

Species Name (i) (or other ID type)	Number of that species in sample	p_i	$\ln(p_i)$	$(p_i)\ln(p_i)$
	_____ Total number from all species on card	This column should add up to 1.00	Refer to natural log table	$H =$ _____ $-$ Sum of all $(p_i)\ln(p_i)$

1. Compare the same species at different sites.

    a. How do the biotic and abiotic factors seem to affect the number of species?

    _____

    _____

    _____

    _____

    b. How do the data suggest that there are species preferences for one type of food over the other? Evaluate the preference for one food compared to another.

    _____

    _____

    _____

    _____

2. Determine the differences in the Index values from one location to another.

    a. Describe what is different between the habitats.

    b. How do you think the moisture, temperature, and any other biotic or abiotic factors influenced your results?

    c. How do the data suggest that there may be a general preference for one type of food over the other? Evaluate the preference for one food compared to another.

    d. Describe how the Index values support your conclusions.

    _____

    _____

    _____

    _____

3. Describe how the Shannon-Weiner Diversity Index could be used to evaluate dinosaur and plant diversity in a Jurassic fossil bed from 150 million years ago and then also be compared to a fossil bed from the Cretaceous of 90 million years ago. Comment on the reliability of proposing theories based on such data.

    _____

    _____

    _____

    _____

    _____

4. Design an experiment by which you could evaluate the effect of an invasive plant species, such as purple loosestrife, on songbird diversity, using the Shannon-Weiner Diversity Index.

_____

_____

_____

_____

_____

Extension

Further develop your study of diversity with the following activity.

Step 1   Cut five different-sized squares of plywood to the following lengths per side:

> 15 cm   50 cm   1.0 m   1.5 m   2.0 m

Plywood is very durable when it rains and can be used year after year.

Step 2   Calculate the surface area of each plywood sheet in square meters and record it on a data table.

Step 3   Set the plywood out in similar locations in close contact with the ground for 5 to seven days.

Step 4   A week later collect all of the invertebrates that you find under each board. (_Lab Hint:_ If possible take a digital picture as soon as you turn the board over, as some creatures will scurry away before they can be counted or collected.)

Calculation

Calculate the Diversity Index for the life forms on each different-sized board. Then describe the apparent effect of habitat size on diversity.

_____

_____

_____

_____

_____

_____

_____

_____

_____

1. Graph your data with the surface area plotted on the *x*-axis and the values of *H* plotted on the *y*-axis.

   a. If you can take advantage of Excel, use the Chart Wizard to plot the data as a scatterplot.

   b. Plot a regression line by clicking on your graph and then going to the Chart menu and selecting Add Trendline.

   c. Look at your graph to determine what type of Trendline or regression you need and select it.

   d. Use Options for displaying the equation for the Trendline and R-squared value, which is a reliability measure.

2. Conduct research on actual data for islands or long peninsulas. Compare your information as graphed to those data. Describe any similar patterns.

INVESTIGATION

19

World Population Growth

PURPOSE

➤ Graph and mathematically analyze the rates of human population growth through history

➤ Project human populations into the future based on generalizations from various data sources for modern times

INTRODUCTION

There is a close connection between the human population of the Earth and many of the problems we currently face as a global society. Issues such as resource depletion, energy consumption, global food supplies, drinking water reserves, soil erosion, water and air pollution, global climate patterns, and many others are directly related to the growing number of people living on our planet.

Fig. 19-1

This long-range population projection, from United Nations sources, focuses on divergent trends between industrialized and less-developed nations.

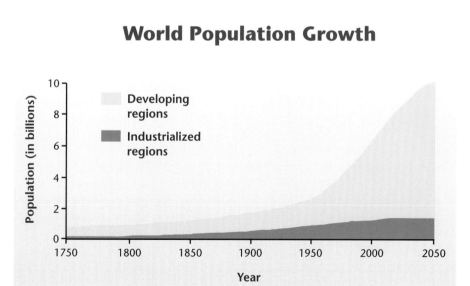

As seen in **Fig. 19-1**, since about 1950 differing population trends between the developing and industrialized regions of the world have further complicated the situation. In this exercise you will examine human growth trends closely and draw conclusions about population numbers—and problems—in the coming generations.

Materials

- graphing paper
- Internet access

Optional:

- Excel software

PART I: Historical Overview and Analysis

Procedure

Step 1   Carefully plot the data given in chart form below. These are good estimates of world populations at various times since the beginning of human civilization.

Year	Population
8000 BC	4 million
4000 BC	7 million
500 BC	100 million
AD 500	200 million
AD 1000	250 million
AD 1500	400 million
AD 1700	600 million
AD 1900	1.6 billion
AD 1950	2.5 billion
AD 1980	4.5 billion
AD 2000	6.1 billion

Step 2   Plot years along the *x*-axis and label this axis Time. Start at 8000 BC, letting each inch equal 1000 years. *Attention:* Set your scales carefully; the data points are *not* uniformly spaced.

Step 3   Label and plot the population, in billions, along the *y*-axis. If you are using graph paper ruled in inches, let each inch equal 1 billion people. Each tenth of an inch then equals 100 million people. *Lab Hint:* Data for the earliest years will be difficult to plot exactly to this scale. If available, metric ruled graph paper is easier to use.

Step 4   Draw a smooth line that *best* connects all the data points.

Step 5   If taking advantage of Excel, use Chart Wizard to plot the data as a scatterplot.

- Plot a regression line by clicking on your graph, then going to the Chart menu and selecting Add Trendline.
- Look at your graph to determine what type of Trendline or regression you need and select it.
- Use Options for displaying the equation for the Trendline and R-squared value, which is a reliability measure.

Laboratory Investigations for AP Environmental Science

1. Examine the shape of the plotted line on your graph.

   a. What type of mathematical relationship exists between human population and time?

_____

   b. Label the regions of the graph that represent the Lag Phase, Exponential Phase, and Stabilization Phase.

   c. Define what is meant by the terms *"J" curve* and *"S" curve*.

_____

_____

_____

2. Analyze the patterns of growth after 2000.

   a. Predict the world's population in the year 2050 and plot it.

   b. If you used Excel, let the program give you the population and plot it for you.

   c. Explain why this value may be realistic. Also give a reason why it may not be.

_____

_____

_____

   d. Describe how three environmental problems we now face would change if your predicted value came true.

_____

_____

_____

_____

3. Estimate as best you can the doubling time for the population after each period:

   a. 8000 BC _____ ?   500 BC _____ ?   1700 _____ ?

      1900 _____ ?   1950 _____ ?   1980 _____ ?   2000 _____ ?

   b. What is the pattern of doubling times?

_____

   c. Using the "Rule of 70," calculate the rate of population growth for each of the above intervals. **Show your calculations.**

Exercises

d. Graph the doubling times over time.

e. Use your graph of doubling times to predict the rate of growth and the population in the year 2050.

_____

_____

PART II: Modern Trend Analysis and Projections

1. Observe this graph of past and projected population growth.

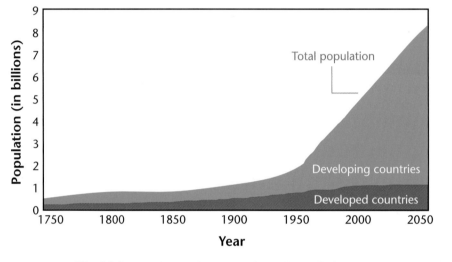

World Population, 1750–2050

Fig. 19-2 **Graph Based on Data from the World Bank**

a. What was the approximate population of the world in 2000?

_____

b. What percent of Earth's people lived in developed countries then?

_____

c. What is the World Bank prediction for world population in 2050?

_____

d. What percent of the world's people will live in developing countries in 2050? What increase is that in the number of people living in developing countries since 2000?

_____

e. The population of the developed world is projected to stabilize just after 2000. Give three reasons why stabilization is not expected in the developing world.

_____

_____

_____

_____

2. Plot the Total Midyear Population data of the U.S. Census Bureau over the period 1950–2050, accessing this site:

http://www.census.gov/ipc/www/worldpop.html

a. How are the World Bank and U.S. Census graphs the same? Different?

_____

_____

b. Why do they seem to disagree?

_____

_____

3. Determine the trends in doubling time for the World Bank and Census Bureau graphs.

a. What population can be expected for 2250, based on World Bank data?

_____

b. What projection do you get from the U.S. Census data for the year 2250?

_____

c. Refer to the United Nations graph at the start of this exercise (**Fig. 19-1**). How do you project the world population for 2250 using that source?

_____

d. Give three possible explanations why these projections differ.

_____

_____

_____

_____

Analysis Problems **Exercises** Questions

4. Look at the graph you made from the data in **PART I**.

    a. Suppose you used those data to make projections like those for Question 2. Explain what problems you would have.

_____

_____

_____

_____

    b. How could you change the scale to allow for a clearer projection?

_____

_____

_____

_____

5a. In general, what do the three graphs imply about the growth of human populations?

_____

_____

_____

    b. Taking into account their differences, what do the graphs all imply about future population growth?

_____

_____

_____

_____

    c. Outline three steps that could be taken to change these growth trends in the developing world.

_____

_____

_____

_____

_____

_____

INVESTIGATION 20

Quantitative

Doubling Time
in Exponential Growth

PURPOSE

➤ Investigate the mathematical concept of exponential growth, applying doubling time as a calculation method

➤ Explore the impacts of exponential growth in biological and other processes

INTRODUCTION

Growing populations of organisms do not follow linear rates of change. One reason populations grow very rapidly is that they have higher birth rates than death rates. Each cycle of reproduction has more offspring than the previous generation. At any point there are more maturing producers than ever before and the increase in the base population accelerates. Mathematically, such growth is called **exponential**. It is the same type of rate as describes compounding interest in a bank account. While the rate is fixed and may be a small percentage, it is continually applied to a growing base, so that the total expands by a greater and greater amount per unit of time.

The time in which a population or money amount *doubles* is a good benchmark by which to grasp and foresee the impact of exponential growth over time. For even the smallest rate of steady growth leads eventually to doubling and redoubling. While exponential growth in one's investments is welcome, when applied to populations, especially human populations, it can have grave implications. Many people do not have a good grasp of exponential rates. The following two exercises will illustrate the powerful effects of exponential growth when it is modeled as a process of doubling, or repeatedly multiplying by two.

Materials

• calculator

• encyclopedias or other sources of global resource data

A math major is home for a vacation break and takes a job for thirty days. In negotiating for a salary, she tells her employer that instead of a wage of $20/hr, she would accept one that pays one penny the first day, then doubles to two cents the next day, four cents the third day, and so on for the month. The employer thinks that this is a good deal for him and agrees.

Show your work, including intermediate calculations.

1. Is this deal a good one for the boss? If so, under what conditions?

2. How is this a good deal for the math major?

3. When does the student break even—that is, on what day has she made as much as she would have earning $20 per hour?

4. What is the total differential in the two payment methods over the 30-day period?

Exercises

Analysis Problems Questions

5. Define exponential growth. Explain why it is so powerful.

6. Describe an example of exponential growth in another field, such as science.

7. Explain what external factors might put limits on this type of mathematical increase.

Problem B

Under ideal conditions some common bacteria can divide and double their numbers in less than one-half hour. Suppose one spring day at 6 A.M., a few such bacteria fall into a can of strawberry syrup in a broken garbage bag behind a snack bar. These conditions—warmth, moisture, and lots of food—are perfect for growth, and the population doubles every 20 minutes. But by 6 P.M. the bacteria are overcrowded and dry and their food is gone.

As you will discover in your calculations, this story about bacteria dramatizes the uncertain state of our natural resources, even in times of perceptible abundance.

Show your work. Explain any assumptions you make.

1. At what time did the can of syrup become half full?

2. At one point during the day some forward-thinking bacteria get the idea that they are facing a crisis. Their numbers are growing exponentially and they are using up their space and food at an ever-increasing rate. At what time do you think that idea would come? Explain.

3. Why would awareness of the crisis not occur before 5 P.M.? How much food remains at that time? (Imagine hearing the bacteria politicians saying: "Don't worry, we still have ¾ of our resources. We have more food than we have ever eaten since we got here.")

4. In spite of the rhetoric, a few bacteria search for more food and space. They find three more syrup cans. How much of a time reprieve are the bacteria given by this find? When will the new cans be depleted?

5. Suppose the global human population growth rate is about 1.3% annually. How long does it take for the human population to double?

6. Given your response to Question 5 and your research into Earth's natural resources, how far along are we in terms of Earth's carrying capacity for humans? Briefly describe the kinds of factors to consider.

7. Thomas Malthus wrote *An Essay on the Principle of Population* in 1798. It had a deep effect on history, influencing Darwin's ideas of evolution. Research this work.

    a. What did Thomas Malthus have to say on the relationship between population growth and our ability to grow food?

_____

_____

_____

_____

    b. Mathematically, Malthus's thesis had a valid basis. Outline three reasons why Malthus' predictions of 1798 have not come true.

_____

_____

_____

_____

    c. Could his predictions come true in the future? Briefly explain.

_____

_____

_____

_____

Exercises

8. To many of us, Earth does not seem crowded. There are vast, undeveloped areas even in the United States. Explain what "part of the can" is left for us, compared to the bacteria.

_____

_____

_____

_____

_____

_____

_____

At this time humans do not have the option of finding "other cans." Earth is all we have. The writer and inventor Buckminster Fuller called it Spaceship Earth, saying we are part of a six billion-member crew flying through an isolated region of space. If we get into trouble, there is no one to help us.

9. Describe three actions you can take as an individual to help us avoid the fate of the bacteria in the first can.

_____

_____

_____

_____

_____

_____

_____

_____

_____

_____

_____

_____

_____

_____

_____

_____

_____

Global Population Trends

PURPOSE

➤ Analyze and compare human population trends in nations of divergent economic development

➤ Factor in the impacts of various historic events on populations to predict future growth and social conditions

INTRODUCTION

In Investigations 19 and 20 you developed mathematical and graphic models to represent and project human population growth. In this project you will analyze human populations by sex, age, and economic development to refine your predictions, based on a variety of possible historical events taking place.

Fig. 21-1

Population pyramids, such as this one for the United States in 2000, break down populations by gender (horizontal axes) and by age group (vertical axes).

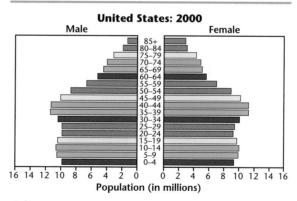

Materials

• Internet access

• encyclopedias or other sources for global economic and political data

Procedure

Access the U.S. Census Bureau Web site at: www.census.gov/ipc/www/idbpyr.html At this site choose any three nations of the world so that you have one in each of these three categories: Developed, Developing, and Underdeveloped. Use the default settings for the three years 2000, 2025, and 2050, then print out your nine population pyramids.

1. Analyzing the pyramids for each of the three countries in turn, discuss why the profile changes as it does over time. Focus on how the pyramid varies in the youngest segments of the population.

2. What patterns do you see in the differences and changes in the male/female ratios?

3. Compare the oldest age group in each of the categories for 2000. Do they change in the same ways for 2025 and 2050? What reasons would you give?

4. Consider how the overall population of each country will fare as time progresses.

   a. Will conditions for the people likely improve or degrade? Explain.

   b. What are the implications for immigration patterns over the 50-year period?

For the remaining questions, make use only of your three pyramids for the year 2000.

5. Using **Fig. 21–2** as a template (see next page), briefly outline how the three total populations, or a certain segment of them, would be impacted by each future event listed in the left column. It would be helpful to research examples of such events in recent history.

Fig. 21-2: Comparison Table for Growth Under Varied Conditions

Event	Developed Country	Developing Country	Underdeveloped Country
Famine			
War			
Lowering of the marital age			
Development of effective birth control			
Outbreak of cholera epidemic			
Severe, chronic air pollution			
Lowering of infant mortality			
Start-up of a social security system			
Economic boom			
Economic depression			
Legislation of child labor laws			
More employment opportunities for women			

Analysis

Problems

Exercises

Questions

6. Select two events that would have the effect of allowing one nation's population to continue to increase rapidly. Briefly explain why the population would continue to rise.

a.

_____

_____

_____

_____

_____

_____

b.

_____

_____

_____

_____

_____

_____

7. Select two factors that would have a stabilizing effect on the population of the same country. Explain why these factors should work in the way you predicted.

a.

_____

_____

_____

_____

_____

_____

b.

_____

_____

_____

_____

INVESTIGATION

22

Population Distribution
and Survivorship

Lab

PURPOSE

➤ Collect data to develop survivorship curves and age-sex population pyramids

➤ Predict characteristics of future populations based on sex, age, fertility, species life cycle, and other factors

INTRODUCTION

Most individuals do not reach the maximum life span of their species, and many die prematurely. The ratio of age at death to the surviving portion of a population is a function of the species and, for human populations, also of the historical period and its socio-economic conditions. A **survivorship curve** shows the probability that an individual of a particular species, age, and gender will survive to a certain age.

Fig. 22-1

Survivorship curves show variations in the relation between the age group in a population and its rate of survivorship. A Type I curve reflects most individuals surviving to maturity and beyond, while Type III curves describe very high early-life mortality followed by a steadying rate of survival.

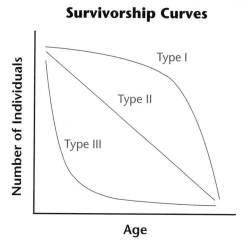

In Part 1 of this lab you will organize actuarial data to produce survivorship curves. A survivorship curve is normally generated by plotting the logarithm of the fraction of individuals surviving against the age of the individual. In your relatively small study, logarithms will not need to be computed. It is possible and often useful to compare the survivorship of different species by stretching or shrinking the *x*-axis so that two or more curves end at the same point, the maximum lifespan for the species. In this lab you will graph and compare the two genders of human populations, choosing one of three possible data collection methods.

In Part 2 of the lab, you will go on to make age-sex diagrams from the same data. This kind of graphing tool is useful to ecologists in predicting the trends of population growth over time.

Materials

- newspaper obituaries *or*
- cemetery access *or*
- Internet access

Optional:
- archives of 19th-century newspapers
- access to a cemetery dating to the 19th century

PART I: Producing a Human Survivorship Curve

Procedures

Method 1: Newspaper Data You will collect data on age of death from obituaries in a local newspaper. Since at least 300 individual obituaries will be needed for a proper distribution, you may start collecting a month or two before organizing the statistics and carrying out the investigation, depending on the size of the circulation area of your local newspaper. Low population areas will have fewer deaths and therefore take much longer to supply data. (Alternatively, you could collect the data by going to the web page of a newspaper covering a larger population region in your state.)

Step 1 From each obituary, record the age at death and sex:

Individual 1:   Age at death _____   Sex _____

Individual 2:   Age at death _____   Sex _____

Individual 3:   *and so on . . .*

To save time and develop a larger sample, the data may be organized by several groups working independently. The information can be accumulated on a single data table for the class and then entered in a spreadsheet.

Step 2 Construct a table that breaks the data into age categories of five-year intervals: 0–4.9, 5–9.9, 10–14.9, etc. Follow that pattern to include the oldest individuals you find. Set up the data table to record, for each sex and age category, **Number of Deaths**, **Total Surviving** to the next age group, and **Mortality Rate**. A chart like that below gives space to record raw data and enter necessary calculations.

Fig. 22-2: Survivorship Data Table

AGE	MALE			FEMALE		
	Number of Deaths	Total Surviving	Mortality Rate	Number of Deaths	Total Surviving	Mortality Rate
20.0+						
15–19.9						
10–14.9						
5–9.9						
0–4.9						

TOTAL _____   TOTAL _____

Step 3 For each sex, calculate the total number of deaths you recorded.

Step 4 To calculate the **Total Surviving** for the first age group, subtract the number of deaths for 0–4.9 years from the total number of deaths for that sex. For the next higher age group, subtract the number of deaths from the number of survivors of the first age group. Continue this pattern until the number of survivors drops to zero. Do this for all the males and then for all the females.

Step 5 To calculate the **Mortality Rate** for each age group in each sex, divide the number of deaths by the total number of individuals of that sex. Note that the rate rises for the older age groups.

Step 6 Develop a survivor curve by first setting the axes: age groups on the *x*-axis and the mortality rates on the *y*-axis. (*Lab Hints:* Set your scales to spread over most of the graph paper. Also, since male and female data will be plotted on the same set of coordinates, the scales must allow for all data from both data sets.)

Step 7 Plot your data for age vs. mortality. Use separate lines of different colors and different point protectors for males and females.

Step 8 **Extension (optional)** Collect data from newspaper archives for obituaries in the 19th century. Repeat the above procedure, then compare the two curves.

Method 2: Cemetery Data This method requires permission to use a cemetery to collect data from headstones. It also requires that respect for the gravesites always be shown. Your class will need information from at least 300 stones. Because cemeteries usually fill up section by section, based on the years that deaths occur, it is important to sample a large enough area to get a representative sample. An advantage of choosing an old cemetery is that you can collect two data sets from different centuries and compare the two curves.

Step 1 Working in pairs, find the following data: year of birth, year of death, and sex. Calculate age by subtracting birth year from death year and record age and sex.

Individual 1:   Age at death _____   Sex _____

Individual 2:   Age at death _____   Sex _____

Individual 3:   *and so on . . .*

To save time and develop a larger sample, the data may be organized by several groups working independently. The information can be accumulated on a single data table for the class and then entered in a spreadsheet.

Step 2 Construct a table that breaks the data into age categories of five-year intervals: 0–4.9, 5–9.9, 10–14.9, etc. Follow that pattern to include the oldest individuals you find. Set up the data table to record, for each sex and age category, the **Number of Deaths, Total Surviving** to the next age group, and **Mortality Rate**. (A chart like that given in **Fig. 22–2** gives space to record raw data and enter necessary calculations.)

Step 3 Calculate the total number of males and females in your class data set.

Step 4 To calculate the **Total Surviving** for the first age group, subtract the number of deaths for 0–4.9 years from the total number of deaths for that sex. For the next higher age group, subtract the number of deaths from the number of survivors of the first age group. Continue this pattern until the number of survivors drops to zero. Do this for all the males and then for all the females.

Step 5 To calculate the **Mortality Rate** for each age group in each sex, divide the number of deaths by the total number of individuals of that sex.

Step 6 Develop a survivorship curve by first setting the axes: age groups on the *x*-axis and the mortality rates on the *y*-axis.
(*Lab Hints:* Set your scales to spread over most of the graph paper. Also, since male and female data will be plotted on the same set of coordinates, the scales must allow for all data from both data sets.)

Step 7 Plot your data for age vs. mortality. Use separate lines of different colors and different point protectors for males and females.

Step 8 **Extension (optional)** Collect data from grave markers for people who died in the nineteenth century and repeat the above procedure. Then compare the two curves.

Method 3: Internet Data If it is not feasible to collect obituary data or to visit a cemetery, then you can gather the required data from a number of Internet Web sites. Consider these:

• The USGenWeb Project, maintained by a volunteer group for genealogy research: http://www.rootsweb.com/~usgenweb
  The Web site has cemetery data broken down by state. From there you can search for information closer to home.

- This page is also broken down by state and includes National Cemeteries: http://www.interment.net/us/index.htm
  The main Web site has records from 7,500 cemeteries around the world. It would be a good twin project to compare survivorship curves from around the world. If interested, discuss pursuing this variation in the lab with your teacher.

- Conduct an Internet search using Google or another search engine and find your own Web sites of data, of which there are many thousands. Some sites will have the information already organized in tabular form, saving some work on your part and allowing for larger or additional samples.

Step 1 Go to the Web site you selected and record age at death and sex for at least 300 individuals, about one-half male and one-half female.

Step 2 Construct a table that breaks the data into age categories of five-year intervals: 0–4.9, 5–9.9, 10–14.9, etc. Follow that pattern to include the oldest individuals you find. Set up the data table to record, for each sex and age category, the **Number of Deaths**, **Total Surviving** to the next age group, and **Mortality Rate**. (A chart like that given in **Fig. 22–2** allows space to record raw data and enter necessary calculations.)

Step 3 Calculate the total number of males and females in your class data set.

Step 4 To calculate the **Total Surviving** for the first age group, subtract the number of deaths for 0–4.9 years from the total number of deaths for that sex. For the next higher age group, subtract the number of deaths from the number of survivors of the first age group. Continue this pattern until the number of survivors drops to zero. Do this for all the males and then for all the females.

Step 5 To calculate the **Mortality Rate** for each age group in each sex, divide the number of deaths by the total number of individuals of that sex.

Step 6 Develop a survivorship curve by first setting the axes: age groups on the *x*-axis and the mortality rates on the *y*-axis.
(*Lab Hints*: Set your scales to spread over most of the graph paper. Also, since male and female data will be plotted on the same set of coordinates, the scales must allow for all data from both data sets.)

Step 7 Plot your data for age vs. mortality. Use separate lines of different colors and different point protectors for males and females.

Step 8 **Extension (optional)** Many Web sites have data for the nineteenth century. Use this information to plot similar curves for populations from those times. Then compare the curves.

1. Compare the survivorship curves for males against those for females.

   a. Explain the differences and why they occur.

   _____

   _____

   _____

   _____

   _____

   _____

   b. Give details of possible biological and social/historical causes. For example, evolutionary theory implies that females in the child-bearing years suffer higher mortality from childbirth deaths. How and in what periods do your data reflect this tendency?

   _____

   _____

   _____

   _____

   c. Describe changes in mortality for males as a result of wars.

   _____

   _____

   _____

2. Analyze and compare the mortality rates for the older age groups.

   a. In general, why should these rates be higher than the average?

   _____

   _____

   b. If you did not make a survivor curve for a nineteenth-century population, predict how it would differ in three ways from the more recent population data you did plot.

   _____

   _____

   _____

   _____

c. If you did plot an additional curve from the nineteenth century, describe and explain how it differs in three ways from the other one you plotted.

_____

_____

_____

_____

3a. How would the survivorship curves of a developed country compare to those of a less developed one?

_____

_____

_____

b. How could survivorship curves be used to make judgments about environmental and health conditions in each of the countries?

_____

_____

_____

_____

4. Humans are generally classified as forming a Type I survivor curve.

    a. What does this fact imply for humans?

_____

_____

_____

    b. Name some other organisms that are generally Type I.

_____

_____

    c. What are the distinguishing characteristics of Type I organisms?

_____

_____

_____

5a. What does it mean to have a Type II survivorship curve?

_____

_____

_____

_____

b. Give two examples of organisms that are generally Type II.

_____

_____

_____

_____

c. Describe how an organism could show characteristics of both Type I and Type II as a reaction to environmental conditions.

_____

_____

_____

_____

_____

_____

6a. What does it mean to have a Type III survivorship curve?

_____

_____

_____

b. Give two examples of organisms that are generally Type III.

_____

_____

_____

c. Describe how an organism could show characteristics of both Type II and Type III as a reaction to environmental conditions.

_____

_____

_____

_____

Analysis

Problems

Exercises

7. If necessary, review the meaning of the terms *r-strategist* and *K-strategist*.

    a. How are the life cycles of these strategists different?

_____

_____

_____

_____

    b. Describe what type of survivorship curves the two should have. Why?

_____

_____

_____

    c. Why do we use the symbols "r" and "K" for these strategies?

_____

_____

_____

    d. Briefly describe an experiment to determine whether an organism is an r- or a K-strategist.

_____

_____

_____

    e. Describe how plants are categorized. How can some be K-strategists? Give an example.

_____

_____

_____

PART 2: Producing Age-Sex Diagrams

Population pyramids, or age-sex diagrams, illustrate the number of people of each sex in a specific five-year age group that are living at a given date. They plot, in bar graph form, the number of males and females in each age group for the total population. Population pyramids are an important model in predicting the future growth of a population. (If you have not carried out Investigation 21, on Global Population Trends, you may wish to review it now for further experience with population pyramid models.)

Fig. 22-3

The overall shape of the bars in an age-sex diagram gives you an image of whether a population is growing, shrinking, or stable at a particular point in time.

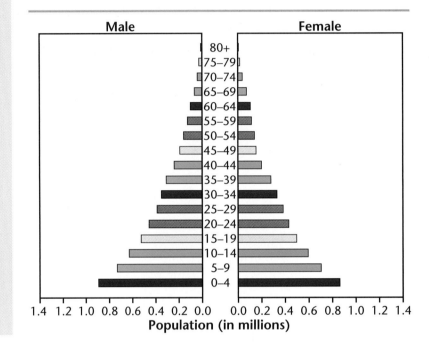

At this point in the investigation you will use the actuarial figures from your survivorship research to draw a population pyramid.

Procedure

Step 1 Using your data table from Part 1, take the number of male and female survivors for each age group. This value represents the number of males and females alive in that age group.

Step 2 Age-sex diagrams have a horizontal axis that plots males on the left side and females on the right side. The vertical axis, with age brackets, normally rises between, although it may be easier to place the scale on the far left. Scale the vertical axis to include all the 5-year age groups for which you collected data in Part 1.

Step 3 Plan the scale of your horizontal axis to match the population data you collected, then plot the data. This scale may represent either the percent of the total population in each group or, as you will give in this case, the absolute population count of the group.

Step 4 The data are plotted out from the middle as a bar graph, one bar per group, as seen in **Fig. 22-3**. You may wish to use color to better distinguish the groups.

1. What pattern of growth does your population pyramid for the more recent data suggest for the future? What evidence makes you formulate that prediction?

_____

_____

_____

_____

2. Analyze how your population pyramid would change in shape if the government built a large military base in the community.

   a. Which age groups would you expect to change the most? Explain.

   _____

   _____

   _____

   _____

   b. Describe two economic impacts the base would have.

   _____

   _____

   _____

   _____

   c. Give two examples of stress on the local environment.

   _____

   _____

   _____

   _____

3. Analyze how the pyramid for a large retirement village would look compared to your pyramid.

   a. What would the differences be? Explain.

   _____

   _____

   _____

   _____

b. Draw what you think the retirement village diagram would look like.

c. How would that retirement population change over time?

_____

_____

_____

_____

_____

_____

d. How would the birth rate and death rate compare to those of your sample?

_____

_____

_____

_____

_____

_____

e. Explain how such a population could remain constant over long periods of time.

_____

_____

_____

_____

_____

_____

_____

4. How would an increase in the fertility rate alter the shape of your pyramid? Why?

_____

_____

_____

_____

_____

5a. Draw a typical population pyramid for a developed country, a developing country, and an underdeveloped country.

b. Describe what type of population change each country could expect over the next 25 years.

_____

_____

_____

_____

_____

c. Explain what the expected quality of life would be in each of those countries if they grew as predicted.

_____

_____

_____

_____

_____

6a. Analyzing the pyramid given in **Fig. 22–3**, predict what will happen to the population of that country over the next 25 years if current trends continue.

_____

_____

_____

_____

b. Why will it change that way?

_____

_____

_____

_____

c. Explain in simple terms if you think such a trend could continue indefinitely.

_____

_____

_____

d. Is this country an economically developed one? Why or why not?

_____

_____

_____

e. What would you predict about this country's use of nonrenewable resources? Why do you postulate that?

_____

_____

_____

f. Comment on the likely situation for employment and education of women in that country.

_____

_____

_____

_____

Project

Energy Resource Comparison

PURPOSE

➤ Research and compare current U.S. electric power production technologies

➤ Outline and defend a power production policy, including feasible alternative technologies, for the coming century

INTRODUCTION

There are many possible approaches to electric power production in the United States. Some of the technologies have long been on line producing power, with various problems and degrees of success and efficiency. As some conventional fuels for these technologies become more scarce and expensive or geopolitically problematic, the need grows to look to the development of alternatives. At the same time the population and its residential and industrial demand for power never cease to expand, creating the need for more generating plants over time.

Fig. 23-1

This power plant generates electricity by burning fossil fuels.

The means of power production listed in the left column of **Fig. 23–2** include conventional fossil fuel-fired plants and nuclear reactors as well as alternative technologies that have the advantage of being renewable. For many of the renewable ones, there remain challenges in implementing their cost-efficient use. Some are in their second and third generation of improvements and yielding some power into the national grid. Some, as of yet, are not practical, but hold great potential for the future. And a few will prove feasible in some parts of the country but not everywhere.

Materials

- Internet access
- encyclopedias and other print sources for information on U.S. electricity generation, fuel sources, and new technologies

Procedure

Based on your texts and any further research that is necessary, fill in the chart. Then, arguing on the basis of factual support, answer the questions that follow.

Fig. 23-2

Energy Resources
Fact Sheet

Energy Source	Availability	State of Technology	Economics	Environmental and Health Considerations
Coal				
Oil				
Natural gas				
Nuclear fission				
Hydroelectric				
Solar				
Wind				
Geothermal				
Nuclear fusion				
Solid waste				
Biomass				
Gas hydrates				
Tidal				
Ocean thermal gradients				

1. Outline a National Energy Policy proposal for producing sufficient electrical power in the United States over the next 100 years. Use separate paper if more space is required.

_____

_____

_____

_____

_____

2. Give the basic rationale for your proposal—why is the new plan imperative? If your plans involve different technologies for different regions, explain why.

_____

_____

_____

_____

_____

3. Compare and contrast your policy to power production today. Explain why it would be in the nation's long-term best interests to alter policy starting now.

_____

_____

_____

_____

_____

4. What would be some economic, environmental, and social benefits of changing to your plan?

_____

_____

_____

_____

_____

Analysis

Problems

Exercises

Quantitative

CO₂ Emissions
from Fossil-Fuel Burning

PURPOSE

➤ Track long-term energy production (1751–2000) and correlate the data to emissions and atmospheric concentrations of CO_2

➤ Investigate the effects of CO_2 and other greenhouse gases on global temperatures

INTRODUCTION

In this investigation you will graph and analyze world-wide energy production historically and its effect on the accumulation of carbon dioxide in the Earth's atmosphere. You will access statistics from the year 1751 and continuing to the near present. The data will also allow you to track the history of technology as humans have proceeded from a mostly coal-burning economy to one exploiting all types of fossil fuel.

Fig. 24-1

Average carbon dioxide (CO₂) concentration in parts per million by volume (ppmv). The data were derived from continuous observations at the Mauna Loa Observatory in Hawaii.

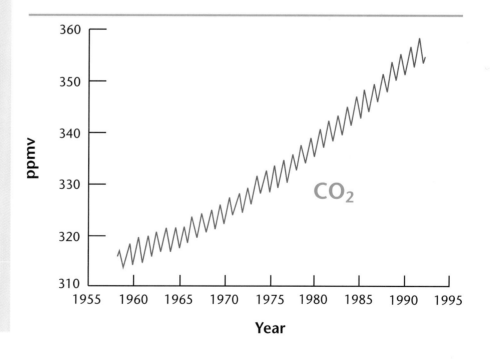

Procedure

Step 1 Go to the following Web site and download the data:
http://cdiac.esd.ornl.gov/ftp/ndp030/CSVFILES/gloal.1751_2000.csv

If this Web site does not load, go to the following site:
http://cdiac.esd.ornl.gov/trends/emis/em_cont.htm

Select **Global**. An option now is to plot data from different parts of the world.

Step 2 You should now have data for about 250 years.

- Set up a graph plotting time on the x-axis and the level of carbon dioxide on the y-axis.

- You may use pencil and paper, TI Interactive or Excel to plot the graphs. The data are comma-delimited and can be cut and pasted into Excel spreadsheet for analysis.

- Set the scales to reflect all the data values you have. (If you use pencil and paper, you may choose to plot just every other or every third data point, or plot only the last 200 years of data.)

Step 3 Plot the values for the three fossil fuels—natural gas, oil, and coal—on the same set of coordinates, using different colored lines.

Laboratory Investigations for AP Environmental Science

1. How do your plots reflect the history of fuel use in the world?

   _____

   _____

   _____

   _____

2. Now plot the per capita data. What do these data imply? Why does the shape of the plotted data look as it does?

   _____

   _____

   _____

3. Suppose the total mass of Earth's atmosphere is about 5.1×10^{18} kg and is about 0.037% CO_2. What was the percent increase in CO_2 as a result of the 2000 emissions?

   Show all your calculations with proper units.

4. Find out where the CO_2 that is produced goes.

   a. Identify and describe some of the carbon dioxide sinks in the natural world.

   _____

   _____

   _____

   b. Describe how humans may be interfering with or inhibiting the sinks.

   _____

   _____

   _____

   c. What is meant by anthropogenic sources?

   _____

   _____

   _____

Questions

5a. Identify and describe the sources of two other greenhouse gases that humans add to the atmosphere.

_____

_____

_____

b. What are their effects on the ability of the atmosphere to hold heat?

_____

_____

_____

_____

c. Compare their heat-holding capacities to that of carbon dioxide.

_____

_____

d. How have their concentrations varied over time?

_____

_____

_____

6. Match the increase in global atmospheric carbon dioxide with temperatures from 1880 to 2000, accessing the following Web page for data:

http://yosemite.epa.gov/oar/globalwarming.nsf/content/climate.html

a. Describe how temperature has varied with the increase of carbon dioxide.

_____

_____

_____

b. Do the data show a direct cause-and-effect relationship? Why or why not?

_____

_____

_____

_____

Laboratory Investigations for AP Environmental Science

Quantitative

Personal Energy Use Audit

PURPOSE

➤ Record and calculate approximate personal energy use in the home today

➤ Compare the amounts, by-products, and dollar costs of competing fuels that are necessary to support personal energy consumption

INTRODUCTION

Electrical consumption has gone up in the United States over the last 50 years for a number of reasons, including increased per capita demand and commercial and industrial demand from economic expansion. While the number of Americans grew by 87 percent from 1950 through 2000 (from under 150 million to almost 280 million), their energy consumption expanded by a much greater 194 percent.

At the same time, some traditional sources of fuel for electrical generation have stagnated or even fallen. In the energy mix today, coal is the dominant fossil fuel for the production of electricity—and growing. In 2001, 51.7% of our electricity was from coal. Petroleum now supplies very little electricity in the U.S., less than previously. Natural gas supplies about 16% of our electricity. Natural gas supply and demand were in relative balance in the United States until the mid-1980s, when a production-consumption gap developed. As a result, in 2001 domestic production of natural gas was 19.7 trillion cubic feet, consumption was 22.2 trillion cubic feet, and imports were 3.98 trillion cubic feet.

Fig. 25-1

One of many thousands of electrical transmission towers in the U.S. energy grid.

Nuclear electric power did not exist in this country until 1957. The new industry expanded rapidly until the 1979 accident at Three Mile Island in Pennsylvania and the Chernobyl catastrophe in Ukraine in 1986. As fewer new units came on line and old units began to shut down, the number of operable units fell to 104 in 2001. Today about 21% of our electricity is from nuclear power, a portion currently in a downtrend.

Our personal use of electricity is very small when compared to the total used in the United States today, and personal consumption of fuels is equally small. But as you have seen in other investigations, when the small amounts used by individuals are added up, they become a very significant value for a large population. Personal decisions about how much energy to use or save and which sources to depend on are very significant.

On the Home Electrical Use chart, **Fig. 25-2**, record the amount of time you use each appliance each day. If an appliance is used a few times a week or less, prorate it to a daily use. If you use any appliances not on the list, determine their power (in watts) by multiplying the volts by the amps on the appliance label. Add these to the list. Convert the watts of power to kilowatts and multiply by the time used to get kilowatt-hours/day.

Fig. 25-2

Home Electrical Use Survey

Appliance	Power (W)	Power (kW)	Number hours/day	Energy/day (kWh/day)
Room AC	1,360			
Clothes washer	512			
Clothes dryer	5,000			
Dishwasher	1,200			
Refrigerator	795			
Blender	300			
Coffeemaker (Drip)	1,100			
Coffeemaker (Perc)	600			
Food Processsor	370			
Hot plate	1,200			
Microwave oven	750			
Mixer	150			
Toaster	1,100			
Computer	60			
Radio	70			
Television	90			
Stereo	125			
VCR	50			
Hair dryer	1,200			
Iron	1,100			
Window fan	200			
Sewing machine	75			
Vacuum cleaner	650			
Light bulb (@75W)	75			
Other				
Other				
TOTALS				

Use the following equivalences in calculating answers to Exercises 1–5. Be sure to show the steps of your work, including set-ups and proper units, as well as final answers.

Conversion Factors

1 kwh = 3.41×10^3 BTU (British Thermal Units)
1 BTU = 2.93×10^4 kWh
1 BTU = 1,055 J (joules)
12,000 BTU = 3.52 kWh = 1.27×10^7 J

1 pound bituminous coal = 12,000 BTU
1 barrel oil = 5.6×10^6 BTU = 5.91×10^9 J
1 ft^3 natural gas = 1,030 BTU = 1.09×10^6 J
1 g ^{235}U = 4.0×10^7 BTU = 4.22×10^{10} J

1. How much electrical energy do you consume each day, on average? How much would that be each year?

2. Suppose the electricity in your region was supplied by the burning of natural gas.

   a. How many cubic feet of natural gas is needed to support your energy lifestyle?

   b. 1,000 ft^3 of natural gas contains about 20.2 kg of methane and when burned completely produces 122 lb of carbon dioxide. How much methane would you consume in one year, and how many pounds of carbon dioxide would you produce?

3. Suppose coal were used in the generators instead of natural gas.

   a. How much coal would be burned to provide your energy?

   b. When coal is burned, about 2.3 lb of CO_2 is produced for every kilowatt of electrical energy consumed. How much carbon dioxide would be produced by your yearly electicity use?

4. Suppose the electrical power was produced by nuclear power. How much uranium would be needed for your yearly consumption?

5. Calculate comparative costs.

    a. The cost for U_3O_8, the primary nuclear reactor fuel, is $10.15 per pound, or about $0.022 per gram. What would be the cost of the uranium to generate your electricity?

    b. Coal costs about $24.38 per ton, and the cost of natural gas for electric utilities, on the average, is about $4.67 per 1,000 cubic feet. Calculate the cost of these two fuels to produce your yearly electricity.

6. Compare the pros and cons of using these fuels to produce electricity on a large scale.

    a. Is the cheapest fuel necessarily the best choice? Explain your reasoning in economic, social, and environmental terms.

_____

_____

_____

_____

_____

    b. Discuss in some detail extraction, processing, transportation, burning, waste products, and health and safety aspects of the problem.

_____

_____

_____

_____

_____

_____

7. Outline five ways to reduce the use of electrical power in your everyday life.

_____

_____

_____

_____

_____

_____

_____

Exercises

Analysis

Problems

Questions

INVESTIGATION 26

Solar Absorption

Lab

PURPOSE

> Design an experiment to calculate and compare the heat-absorbing capacities of various fluids under solar radiation
> Determine efficient applications and models for fluid solar-energy collectors, based on experimental results
> Compute heat absorption rates for passive solar materials

INTRODUCTION

As our supplies of fossil fuels become more difficult to find and extract, alternate sources of energy need to be exploited. It would be best if these sources were renewable and nonpolluting. One constant source of direct energy is the Sun. There are a few ways that solar energy can be utilized. One method, called **passive solar**, is to allow sunlight to be absorbed directly by a material such as stone, brick, or concrete on exposed interior walls, heating buildings without the need for pumps or other machinery. Another method is to let a liquid, such as water, absorb the solar energy and then circulate the heated water through a conventional hot water heating system. A completely different approach to solar energy converts the rays of the sun directly into electricity with the use of **photovoltaic cells**. All these methods use sunlight and convert it into useful energy for us to exploit. Heating solids and liquids to warm buildings is clean and competitive with conventional heating methods. Photovoltaic cells are also becoming competitive in certain applications.

Fig. 26-1

One-Thousand-Year-Old Passive Solar-Heated Homes in Mesa Verde, Colorado

Directly or indirectly, almost all our energy sources are a form of solar energy. Even though the sun is about 93 million miles away, the amount of solar radiation reaching Earth's surface in a few weeks is equal to the energy in the world's reserves of fossil fuels. On average, the upper atmosphere receives 1.37 kWh of energy per square meter each second. This is equivalent to almost 5 million joules/m²/s, or 2 cal/cm²/min.

The effect of this energy on a given surface area of Earth is dependent on many factors, such as actual distance from the sun, the latitude, and the local weather. Certainly not all this solar energy arrives at Earth's surface. Some of it is reflected directly back into space, and some is absorbed by dust, water vapor, and ozone in the upper atmosphere. About 47% of the energy is available at the surface for us to utilize. It has been estimated that if the solar energy hitting the land area of New Jersey, the fourth smallest state, were converted at 20% efficiency, it would meet all our energy needs at present day use rates.

The development of efficient absorbing materials is vital to developing economical solar energy. All materials have an ability to absorb heat. This heat can be quantified as the **specific heat**, which is the amount of heat, in calories or joules, needed to raise the temperature of one gram of material 1 degree C. In this investigation you will design an experiment to explore the ability of various liquids and solutions to collect solar energy.

Materials

- 150 mL beakers
- heat lamp
- pure water
- vegetable oil
- ethanol
- ethylene glycol (automotive antifreeze)

Procedure Suggestions

Step 1 Design an experiment to test at least five different liquids and/or solutions for their heat-holding capacity. Include the four substances listed above. Since darker substances are usually better at absorbing heat, you may want to mix different food coloring agents into some liquids. (Controls of uncolored substances will be necessary if you decide to test for coloring agents.) You can also test varying concentrations of salt solutions.

Step 2 Write out a concise set of directions that can be used if someone else wanted to repeat your experiment.

Step 3 Set up a table of data to record your measurements. You will report the initial and final temperatures along with the temperature change for each liquid. You will also need the time, in hours, that the fluids were exposed to the light source.

Step 4 Use 100 mL of each liquid or solution in a 150-mL beaker. Measure the mass of each liquid by weighing the beaker empty and then again after adding the liquid and subtracting the two values.

Step 5 Ideally, place your beakers in direct sunlight. If this is not possible, then use a heat lamp or other lamp placed about 1 ft above the beakers. Leave the beakers in the light for at least one class period. Convert this time to hours for the data table.

1. Assume all the energy the fluids absorbed was from the top surface. Calculate the surface area of each beaker. (You will have to do this only once if the beakers are of the same size.)

2. Calculate the heat absorbed by each fluid, including any control. The formula is:

$$q = mc\Delta t$$

where q is the heat in joules, m is the mass of the liquid or solution, c is the specific heat of the liquid, and Δt is the temperature change.

The specific heat is a measured constant for each substance. For this experiment, assume that all the water solutions have the same value as pure water.

Substance	Specific Heat
Pure Water	4.18 J/g/C
Vegetable Oil	2.0 J/g/C
Ethanol	2.46 J/g/C
Ethylene Glycol	2.2 J/g/C

3. Compute the number of joules absorbed by each fluid per hour.

4. Using the values calculated in the preceding computations, determine the number of joules per square meter per second (J/m²/s) absorbed on the surface of your fluids.

5. From your data and calculations, which fluid was the best absorber, and which one was the least effective? What is the percent difference between the two?

6. Suppose you were designing a solar collector to be 50 m² (about one-half the surface of an average roof), facing south, and filled with your best absorber fluid. Based on your calculations, determine the following:

   a. How much heat would the collector absorb in one hour?

   b. How much heat would it collect on an ideal sunny day? (Assume that in much of the United States the Sun shines for about 8 hours in winter.)

   c. In a typical house using 80 kilojoules per hour, what percent of the heat needs would the collector produce?

7. Passive solar heating usually utilizes walls of concrete, brick, or stone to absorb the rays of the Sun during the day and then to re-radiate that heat back into the room during the time the Sun does not shine. Concrete can absorb 0.88 megajoules per square meter per degree change in Celsius temperature.

   How much heat could a concrete wall that is 3 meters high and 8 meters long absorb if its temperature changed 8°C?

8. Some hydrated salts, such as sodium sulfate decahydrate ($NaSO_4 \cdot 10H_2O$), are used as a method for storing the energy for periods of extended sunless days. Describe one method of utilizing this technique.

_____

_____

_____

_____

Particulate Air Pollution

PURPOSE

➤ Measure particulate matter locally and evaluate the data by EPA standards

INTRODUCTION

Particulate matter is a term used to describe solid and liquid particles found suspended in the air. The particles have a wide variety of stationary and mobile sources and, therefore, a diverse set of physical and chemical properties. Particulate matter comprises a wide range of substances including road dust, wood smoke, fly ash, diesel soot, and sulfate aerosols. Most of these come from burning fossil fuels for transportation, power generation, and industrial boilers.

Particles in the air range in size, from smoke and soot particles that are dark and large enough to see to particles so small an electron microscope is needed. The smaller particles are the greater health hazard because they can penetrate more deeply into the respiratory tract. Since 1987 the EPA standard for particulate matter is PM-10, which includes particles with a diameter of 10 micrometers or less.

The major health problems from exposure to PM-10 are trouble with breathing, damage to lung tissue, cancer, and early death. The populations most affected by PM-10 are the very young, the elderly, and those with lung disease and asthma. New scientific evidence suggests that particles smaller than 2.5 micrometers can cause serious health problems. The World Health Organization (WHO) has done long-term studies that show the risk of premature death has a threshold of annual concentrations of PM-2.5 of 10 g/m^3. The EPA is reviewing possible changes in the existing PM-10 standard.

Materials

- petri dishes (5)
- petroleum jelly
- hand lens (or low-power microscope)
- wax pencil or marker pen

Procedure

Step 1   Write your name on the outside of five petri dish bottoms. Then, using a quarter as a guide, draw a circle on the inside bottom of the dishes.

Step 2   Carefully smear a thin layer of petroleum jelly inside the circles you drew. Then quickly place the tops of the petri dishes over the bottoms to keep the petroleum jelly clean until you are ready to start your collecting.

Step 3   Keep one petri dish as a control and place the others at various places around the school building and grounds. (If you want to try a few at other locations, discuss with your teacher.)

Step 4   In your lab notes carefully describe the location of each petri dish and any factors that may affect your collecting. Hypothesize what your findings will be at each site, or at least rate the sites in order of the number of particles you expect to find.

Step 5   Set your petri dishes out at the locations you selected and uncover them. After 24 to 48 hours retrieve the petri dishes by immediately covering them. Bring them back to the classroom or lab.

Step 6   For your analysis, uncover a petri dish and using a hand lens or low-power microscope, count the actual number of particles you see caught in the petroleum jelly. Repeat this for all five dishes, including the control. Record the number of particles counted on your data sheet.

Step 7   For each petri dish, try to identify the types of particles and their probable source.

1. The diameter of the quarter gives an area of almost 5 cm². Calculate the approximate number of particles that would be collected if the surface area of your experiment were 1 m².

2. In Problem 1 you calculated the particles in an area of 1 m². PM-10 is measured in micrograms per cubic meter and cubic meters are a measure of volume.

   a. Devise a method to determine the mass of the particles in a volume of air.

   _____

   _____

   _____

   _____

   _____

   _____

   _____

   _____

   _____

   _____

   b. Estimate how your samples would compare to the EPA national air quality standard of 150 μg/m³ (measured as a daily rate).

   _____

   _____

   _____

   _____

   _____

   _____

   _____

   _____

   _____

   _____

3. Are the particles you found considered to be pollution? Why or why not?

_____

_____

_____

_____

_____

_____

_____

_____

4. Outline some procedures to reduce the amount of particulate matter in the areas tested.

_____

_____

_____

_____

_____

_____

_____

_____

_____

_____

Laboratory Investigations for AP Environmental Science

INVESTIGATION

28

Acid Rain

PURPOSE

➤ Measure and compare pH levels in precipitation at several sites over an extended time period

➤ Analyze and account for varying concentrations of oxides and pH readings in precipitation

INTRODUCTION

Acid rain is a general term that describes how acids fall out of the atmosphere. A better term would be **acid deposition**, which occurs two ways: wet and dry. Acid rain, fog, and snow are known as wet deposition. Dry deposition is made up of acidic gases and particles, and these constitute about 50% of all acidic fallout from the atmosphere. The particles get blown by the wind onto cars, buildings, bridges, forests, etc. When it rains, these particles dissolve in the water, and the runoff becomes more acidic than the rainfall itself.

Fig. 28-1

The Sources and Kinds of Acid Deposition

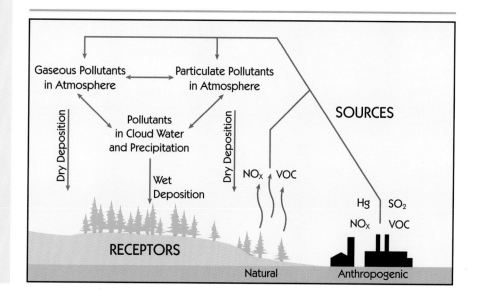

Scientists have documented that oxides of nitrogen and sulfur are the main source of acid rain. About one-fourth of the oxides of nitrogen (NO_x) and two-thirds of the sulfur dioxide come from using fossil fuels, coal in particular, for the generation of electric power. These gases chemically react with and combine with the water and other chemicals in the atmosphere to form dilute solutions of nitric and sulfuric acids. These chemicals mix in the atmosphere and drift with the prevailing winds to be deposited many miles away. The chemicals often cross state and sometimes international borders.

Even if there were no humans on Earth to alter the atmosphere, rainfall would still be acidic because atmospheric carbon dioxide and water combine to form carbonic acid, which has a **pH** of about 5.6. Remember that pH is a measure of the acidity of solutions on a logarithmic scale. It ranges from the very strongly acidic 0, to the neutral 7 of pure water, to very strongly alkaline 14. Tomato juice has a pH of 4 and vinegar and stomach acid have a pH of 3. Precipitation with a pH less than 5 is considered acid rain.

Materials

- beakers (1 per precipitation sample)
- pH meter (or CBL and pH probe, or titrant)
- Internet access

Procedure

Step 1 Wait for a day when it starts to rain or snow, preferably a storm of some duration. To get the maximum effect, it is best to begin this lab on the first day of precipitation.

Step 2 Take very clean, dry beakers and set them outside away from any buildings and trees to collect precipitation. If you are collecting snow, let the beaker fill up, so as to have enough liquid when the snow melts. (If necessary, add snow to the beaker, using a clean scoop and taking only snow from the upper layer that has fallen.)

Step 3 Bring the beakers into the classroom or lab for testing.

Step 4 Use a pH meter or other method to measure the pH of the precipitation. Record your values.

Step 5 Repeat the collection process for different times during the storm, possibly an hour apart.

Step 6 Conduct identical tests for several rainfalls or snowstorms over several months and compare the results.

1. How did the pH values compare as the storm progressed? Why?

_____

_____

_____

_____

2. How did the values compare over the more extended period of time? Why?

_____

_____

_____

_____

_____

3a. What is the primary source of sulfur dioxide emissions?

_____

_____

_____

b. Describe three ways these emissions can be lowered.

_____

_____

_____

_____

_____

_____

c. Study **Fig. 28-2**. Why are the highest values in the Midwest in southeast Ohio?

_____

_____

d. Why are the values so low west of the Rocky Mountains?

_____

_____

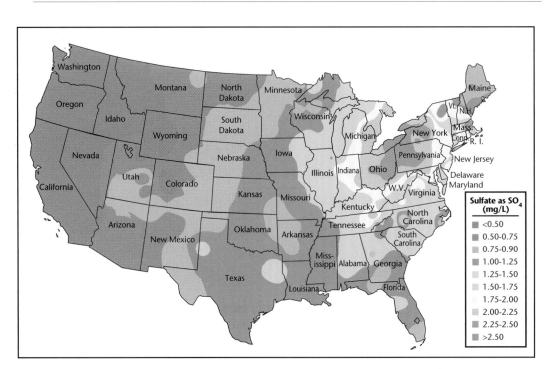

Fig. 28-2: Atmospheric Sulfate Concentrations in the U.S. for the Year 2000 (in mg/L)

4a. What is the primary source of NO_x emissions?

_____

_____

b. Use **Fig. 28-3** (see next page). Where are the highest concentrations on this map, and why?

_____

_____

c. Why are the values so low in rural central and northern California but higher east of the urban San Francisco Bay area?

_____

_____

Laboratory Investigations for AP Environmental Science

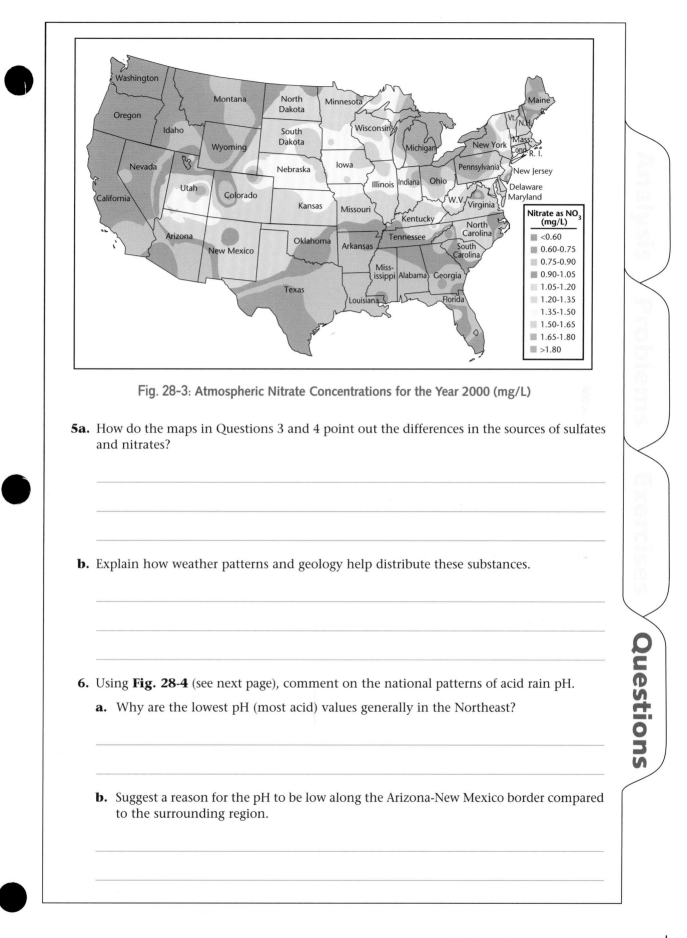

Fig. 28-3: Atmospheric Nitrate Concentrations for the Year 2000 (mg/L)

5a. How do the maps in Questions 3 and 4 point out the differences in the sources of sulfates and nitrates?

_____

_____

_____

b. Explain how weather patterns and geology help distribute these substances.

_____

_____

_____

6. Using **Fig. 28-4** (see next page), comment on the national patterns of acid rain pH.

　a. Why are the lowest pH (most acid) values generally in the Northeast?

_____

_____

　b. Suggest a reason for the pH to be low along the Arizona-New Mexico border compared to the surrounding region.

_____

_____

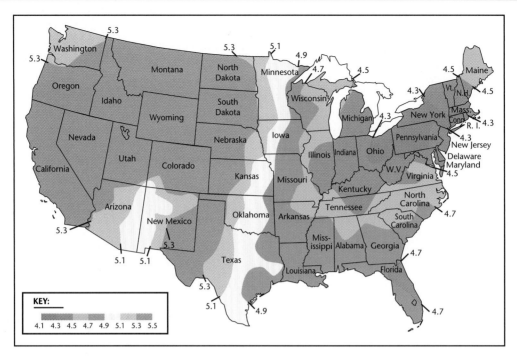

Fig. 28-4: **Acidic Concentrations in Rainfall in the U.S. for 1992**

7. Describe four ways acid rain hurts the economy of the United States.

8. One market-based incentive for reducing pollution is called Tradable Emissions Limitations, or emissions trading for short. The approach used by the EPA is called Allowance Trading, or cap and trade. Research current approaches to reducing industrial pollution and prepare a brief report addressing these topics:

- How does the EPA's allowance trading work for sulfur dioxide trading?
- Where has this approach been tried, and why was that area selected?
- How effective is the program?

Laboratory Investigations for AP Environmental Science

INVESTIGATION
29

Lab

Bioassay Experiment

PURPOSE

➤ Conduct a controlled experiment to test the toxicity of salt on the growth of lettuce seeds

➤ Apply the experimental results to environmental problems

➤ Design a bioassay experiment

INTRODUCTION

The use of a biological organism to test the toxicity of a chemical compound is termed **bioassay**. In this method it is assumed that a test organism will react in a predictable way to increasing amounts of a particular chemical compound. Bioassay has been used by drug companies to test new products on laboratory animals before humans. Bioassays are also used in environmental testing. They can determine the degree of harm to be expected from toxic soil, industrial effluents, agricultural runoffs, dredge spoils, and drilling and mining wastes, as well as to test for the effectiveness of the clean-up of a contaminated site.

In this investigation you will perform what is called a **dose/response experiment**. This method requires you to increase the dose of a chemical incrementally and record how the organism responds to the exposures. For a test organism, you will use lettuce seeds, the Buttercrunch variety if it is available. Lettuces are commonly used in bioassays, along with millet, because their root growth, rather than just germination rate, is especially sensitive to many chemicals. For a variety of reasons salt solutions will be the toxin. Salt is inexpensive and safe to use, and, as you learned in your investigation of soil salinization, it is a widespread environmental problem for plants.

Materials

- lettuce seeds (preferably Buttercrunch)
- salt
- graduated beaker (1 per group)
- petri dishes (10 per group)
- bleach

- filter paper
- distilled or deionized water
- sealable bag (1 large)
- semi-log graph paper

Optional:
- Excel spreadsheet

Procedure

Step 1 Make salt water solutions that are the following percents by volume:
3%   2.5%   2%   1.5%   1%   0.5%   0.1%   0.05%   0.01%
Each lab group can make 100 mL of one solution and share with the other groups.

Step 2 Label 10 petri dishes with your name and the salt concentration. Nine will be test solutions and one will be the control with distilled or deionized water.

Step 3 Place a piece of filter paper on the bottom of each petri dish. (You can also use a piece of fresh paper towel cut to size.)

Step 4 Soak your lettuce seeds in a solution of bleach for 10–15 minutes to kill off any fungus that may interfere with the results of the experiment. Rinse the seeds thoroughly 3–5 times in distilled or deionized water.

Step 5 Place 10 lettuce seeds on the paper in the bottom of each petri dish. Make sure there is a separation between each seed.

Step 6 Cover the seeds with another piece of filter paper or paper towel.

Step 7 Soak the seeds in each petri dish with the appropriate salt solution. Be careful not to let standing liquid solution accumulate on the bottom of the dish. Add just enough solution to moisten the paper tops and bottoms.

Step 8 Add distilled or deionized water to the control petri dish.

Step 9 Seal all 10 petri dishes in a large sealable bag labeled with your name. Put the bag in a dark place at room temperature for 5 days.

Step 10 Make a table of data to include
- the number of seeds that germinated,
- the percent germination,
- the average length of the root, called the **radicle**.

Step 11 After 5 days, open the sealable bag and start to collect your data. Count how many seeds in each petri dish germinated and measure the radicle in millimeters. Be sure that you measure only the root, from the seed remnant to the tip of the root, not the shoot and beginnings of leaves.

Step 12 Calculate the average radicle length for each petri dish and record these data in your data table.

Step 13 Graph the average length of the radicle against salt solution strength on semi-log graph paper. The salt solutions will be plotted logarithmically. (This can be done with pencil and paper or using a spreadsheet like Excel.)

Step 14 On the same graph, plot the percent germination versus the salt solution strength. To do this, make another *y*-axis on the right end of the *x*-axis.

1a. What is meant by the term *threshold of toxicity*? In what other contexts have you seen this term used?

_____

_____

_____

_____

b. On your graph of percent germination vs. solution strength, label the Threshold of Toxicity.

2a. What is meant by *LD-50*? Describe some situations in which it is used.

_____

_____

_____

_____

b. Label LD-50 on your graph of percent germination vs. solution strength.

3. Discuss the three environmental effects of using sodium chloride (NaCl) on roads and highways during ice and snow storms.

_____

_____

_____

_____

_____

_____

4. A common homeowners' substitute to sodium chloride for de-icing driveways and sidewalks is calcium chloride, $CaCl_2$. Using your background knowledge of *colligative* properties from chemistry, explain why calcium chloride should be a more effective de-icing agent.

_____

_____

_____

_____

_____

_____

_____

Problems

5. Water solutions of toxins are usually dilute, making it difficult to use them in a bio-assay. Sediments, especially silty ones, make a very good test medium because they can be thousands and sometimes millions of times more contaminated than water. Outline a bioassay procedure to test the toxicity of a contaminated sediment using lettuce seeds as the test organism.

_____

_____

_____

_____

_____

_____

_____

_____

_____

_____

6. Suppose you had to design the bioassay of a potentially toxic material with which you are not familiar. How would you decide on the number and intervals of concentrations to test? How would you determine the starting and final concentrations?

_____

_____

_____

_____

_____

_____

_____

_____

_____

_____

_____

_____

INVESTIGATION

30

Solid Waste Collection

PURPOSE

➤ Quantify and analyze household solid waste

➤ Propose general strategies for reduction and recycling of solid waste

INTRODUCTION

We live in a throwaway society. Many of the things we buy are designed to be used once and then discarded—everything from beverage bottles to disposable lighters to cameras. More and more products of convenience are on the market. Many come wrapped in multiple layers of wax paper, Styrofoam, cardboard, aluminum foil, paper, or plastic. Available space for landfills is declining, and our society must look for alternatives.

Fig. 30-1

Small amounts add up. More than half the 6,000 municipal sanitary landfills in the U.S. are full and closed.

As our population grows, we consume ever more resources. At the same time, the population finds itself more densely packed as it becomes more urban and suburban, making it more and more difficult to dispose of all the solid waste. About 46 million tons of trash is produced in California alone. That is enough trash to fill a landfill 100 feet wide by 50 feet high and 800 miles long. Per capita, Americans generate more than twice as much trash as people in other developed countries such as Germany and Japan. This investigation looks at the amount of waste you or your family accumulates in a week.

Procedure

Step 1 For one week sort and identify all the trash your family produces. Daily, measure the volume of all:

- paper
- plastic
- metal
- cardboard
- clothes and textiles
- yard waste
- glass
- kitchen/food waste
- any other disposed materials

Record this information in a table. (**CAUTION:** Wear rubber gloves. Take health precautions recording products such as diapers, which can be measured *before* use.)

Step 2 Approximate large volumes by using buckets or pails of known volume, 1–5 gallons for example. A smaller container can be used for food stuffs.

Step 3 Bottles, cans, and other containers should be placed loosely in the measuring container to simulate how they would settle in a landfill.

1. Which materials had the greatest volume? List them in decreasing order by volume.

_____

_____

2. Estimate what percentage of your waste is from redundant packaging.

_____

3. What percent of your waste could be recycled? How much of your family's refuse gets recycled on a regular basis?

_____

4. How can you reduce the amount of waste that cannot be recycled?

_____

_____

5. Assume that your percents of trash types are typical of all families in your locale, and that 50% of the families reduced their trash by recycling all that could be recycled. What would be the volume saved from going into the landfill? Show your math.

6. Describe three effects of landfill on the environment. Are these all harmful? Explain.

_____

_____

_____

_____

_____

7. How does the Tragedy of the Commons exemplify the problem of household waste disposal?

_____

_____

_____

_____

_____

Questions

8. Outline two economic incentives from government to encourage recycling waste.

_____

_____

_____

_____

9. We do not have the luxury of creating ever-more landfills. Outline three viable alternatives to sanitary landfills to solve the problem of disposing of household waste.

_____

_____

_____

_____

10. How can the three "Rs" of Reduce, Reuse, and Recycle be applied to the problem of your household trash?

_____

_____

_____

_____

_____

_____

_____

11. One way of reducing any type of pollution is to turn the waste into a saleable, profit-making product. Describe one method for a trash-collecting agency to make a profit by turning the household waste into a commodity.

_____

_____

_____

_____

_____

_____

_____

INVESTIGATION

31

Auto *and* Truck Tires *and* the Environment

PURPOSE

➤ Calculate the energy available from burning tires to generate electricity

➤ Compute reductions in sulfur dioxide emissions from burning tires in place of coal for cement production

➤ Propose ways of conserving and reusing tires

INTRODUCTION

Drivers in the United States discard approximately 280 million tires per year, and the total number of cast-off tires now approaches 3 billion. When these tires are discarded, they collect water and breed mosquitoes, which can spread diseases such as malaria, St. Louis encephalitis, West Nile virus, and dengue. Even when buried, tires can work their way back to the surface.

Most tire piles are outdoors on open ground, where they pose a serious fire hazard. A tire pile in Winchester, Virginia, burned for nine months in 1983. In this fire, 7 million tires burned for 275 days, and 690,000 gallons of oil

Fig. 31-1

Most states have programs to remove the billions of tires that have been stockpiled in tire piles or just abandoned across the countryside.

running off from the fire were collected and sold for $184,000. One of the largest sites, in Stanislaus County, California, had tires piled as high as six stories. In 1991 it held over 30 million tires. By 1999 it was down to about 7 million tires when lightning started a fire that burned for over a month. Fire would not ever have started at a tire pile near Hamden, Connecticut, where 15 million tires are stored underwater in a flooded quarry—an approach that also prevents breeding of mosquitoes.

One way to remove a pollutant or waste product from the environment is to make it into a profitable commodity. There have been many creative ways to use old tires in an attempt to reduce tire piles. Tires have been used in the making of artificial reefs off the coasts of New Jersey and Delaware. They have been ground up into pieces, called crumb rubber, that are a few millimeters in diameter and used for stabilizing hillsides and as a conditioner for soils, increasing the soil porosity and improving plant root growth. Crumb rubber is mixed with paving asphalt to improve the durability of highways. Whole tires and crumb rubber are used as fuels for power plants and cement manufacturing. There are many other uses for this overlooked resource.

Fig. 31-2

California Tire Diversion Rates (in millions)

The California Integrated Waste Management Board—2003

Year	Estimated Number of Tires Generated	Reused	Recycled	Retreaded	Tires to Fuel	Number of Tires Diverted	Percent Tires Diverted
1997	33.2	1.5	5.4	2.8	9.0	_____	_____
1998	33.8	1.5	9.1	2.8	7.5	_____	_____
1999	34.0	2.4	10.1	2.5	7.9	_____	_____
2000	34.5	3.6	13.0	2.4	5.2	_____	_____
2001	34.8	1.5	14.9	2.4	5.2	_____	_____

Reused — Tires that have a lot of tread left and can be resold as used tires.

Recycled — Tires mostly ground up into "crumbs" and reused in many applications.

Retreaded — Tires with good sidewalls, processed to get a new tread surface. (Air Force One, most buses and taxis, and a high percentage of trucks all safely use retreads.)

Tires to Fuel — Tires that are burned, either as whole tires in the making of cement or as crumbs in power plants. They can also be processed into oil to burn industrially.

Tires Diverted — The total number of tires removed from the piles by reusing, recycling, retreading, or burning as a fuel.

Percent Diverted — The percent of all the tires removed from the piles.

1. As seen in the Tire Diversion chart, **Fig. 31-2**, recycling is the most efficient method of reducing old tires in recent years in California. Complete the chart, using the description of the various columns.

    a. Plot the percent of tires recycled compared to the total number of tires generated each year.

    b. Project what the percent recycled would be in 2004.

2. One tire can generate about 250,000 BTUs. The average American home consumes about 10,000 kilowatt-hours per year. Assume one BTU equals about 3×10^{-4} kWh and production of electricity from tires is 60% efficient.

    a. How many tires would be needed to supply the 10,000 kWh per year?

    b. Suppose 30% of the tires discarded in California in 2001 were burned for electric power at 60% efficiency. How many homes would that supply with electricity?

    c. Assume 1 pound of coal produces 12,000 BTUs. How many tons of coal would be saved by using the tires instead of coal as the energy source? (1 ton = 2,000 lb)

3. Whole tires can be used as the energy source in kilns that make cement by heating limestone to over 2,500° F. At temperatures that high, no toxins are released, and the steel in the bead and belts of the tires is converted to iron oxide, which is necessary in the making of cement. Any small amount of ash that would be released is incorporated into the cement. By this process, a single kiln can use 2 million tires per year, saving more than 2 gallons of oil, or 25 pounds of coal, per tire used.

One ton of coal produces 80 pounds of sulfur dioxide, a major cause of acid rain. But tires have much lower sulfur concentrations than coal. By using tires in a cement kiln instead of coal, how many tons of sulfur dioxide are kept out of the environment?

4. One way to keep tire piles from being a problem is by conservation. By allowing our tires to last longer, they do not need to be replaced so quickly. The major cause of increased tread wear is underinflation. Driving on a tire that is 20% underinflated can reduce the life of the tire by almost 10,000 miles. It also lowers the fuel economy of your vehicle by 4–5%.

   a. The average normal tire will drive 45,000 miles. If the tire is 20% underinflated, how far can it be driven under otherwise normal conditions?

   b. Assume the average driver puts 15,000 miles a year on his tires. There are about 140 million cars in the United States. If 50% of them had on tires 20% underinflated, how many extra tires would be needed?

5. Last year, about 30 million tires were shredded for civil engineering projects.

   a. Describe how shredded tires can be used as a soil conditioner for athletic fields and golf courses.

   _____

   _____

   _____

   b. Identify and explain two other uses for shredded tires.

   _____

   _____

   _____

Political Activism Letter

Project

PURPOSE

➤ Investigate the environmental issue of whether to drill for oil and gas in the Arctic National Wildlife Refuge (ANWR) in northeastern Alaska

➤ Write a letter to a nationally elected government official, urging him or her to take a specific action on this issue

INTRODUCTION

It is important to tell elected officials where you stand on issues and that you are an active, interested voter. Your input on clean water, urban sprawl, energy, trade, and other issues can help shape the way your representatives create and implement environmental and social policy. E-mails, postcards, and faxes are good communication tools, but letters and phone calls are the most effective and persuasive way of communicating your views to elected officials. They show that you are willing to do extra work to convey your ideas and that you are more committed than someone who simply sends blind bulk mailings or other mass-market types of communiqué.

Fig. 32-1

The United States Capitol

To write an effective letter arguing for or against opening ANWR to drilling, you must provide the official with background information. You need to explain why he or she should go along with your view. This requires objective thought and research. As an example, the May 2001 issue of Scientific American has an excellent balanced article describing many of the issues involved in this complex problem. There are many other sources in the literature and on the Web. Much of what is written is very biased, so be careful of your sources.

Procedure

Step 1 Research the topic. In preparation, develop responses to all the "Points to Ponder" raised in the last section of this project.

Step 2 Draft your letter. These tips will help you write a more persuasive letter:

- Keep it short. Limit your letter to one page and one issue.
- Identify yourself as a concerned, motivated, and involved new voter. Do not refer to the letter as a school project.
- Be polite, but take a firm position. Be confident in your understanding of the issue, and remember that the legislator may know less than you and may be voting along party lines or with the polls.
- If you are writing to a senator or representative, cite the specific bill and identify it by number. You can access the Congressional Web site to find the bill numbers for and against opening ANWR.
- Clearly describe the issue and your view of it. Select just three or four of the strongest scientific reasons that support your argument and develop them clearly. Too much information can distract from your position.
- After stating arguments, make the letter personal. Say why the issue matters to you and how it affects you, your family, and your community. Make a connection to the legislator. Outline where you agree with him or her on other issues and how this one is very important personally.
- Always thank politicians for their time and efforts on your behalf and urge them to see your point of view. (If they vote the way you want, send them a thank-you note. This may help if you write again, on another issue.)

Step 3 Check over your letter. Remember to:

- Request a *specific* action, whether to open ANWR to drilling or not.
- Ask for a reply. Include your name and address on your letter and envelope.
- Include an envelope with your typed return address (don't seal this!)
- Provide the background information that you used to formulate your argument. If a document is from the Internet, underline the most important points. Do not include multiple-page print-outs—just key excerpts.

- Make a bibliography documenting all reliable or authoritative sources you used, such as an informative map or the Scientific American article.

Step 4 Address your letter to one elected official with correct title and address. Contact

The president at:	The White House 1600 Pennsylvania Avenue N.W. Washington, D.C. 20500
Your senator at:	U.S. Senate Washington, D.C. 02510
Your representative at:	House of Representatives Washington, D.C. 02515

Or look them up online at:

http://www.congress.com/

Before you write your letter, consider the following topics and ideas. By having answers to them, you will be better able to summon good arguments. To carry out your research, try the Web sites listed after the questions.

Points to Ponder for your Letter

1. Estimates are that at a price of $24/barrel, there are 7 billion barrels that could be economically extracted in ANWR. If the price fell to $18/barrel, there would be only 5 billion barrels that could be extracted at a profit, and if the price plummeted to $12/barrel, there would be only a few hundred million barrels.

   If we start to drill in ANWR, could OPEC undermine our efforts by increasing their production and lowering the price of a barrel of oil enough to make it unprofitable for us to continue drilling? What would be the implications of a start without follow-up?

   _____

   _____

   _____

2. Refer to **Fig. 32-2**. Those in favor of drilling say that 1002 Area is a very small percentage of the land area of Alaska and even a small percentage of the Arctic National Wildlife Refuge (1.5×10^6 out of 19.5×10^6 acres, or 7.7%). By this fact they imply that such a very small area does not compare to all of the natural beauty and wildlife that abounds in Alaska. Consider:

   a. Why might it be a bad idea to drill in this tiny spot?

   _____

   _____

   _____

   _____

   b. What else happens on this disputed coastal plain? Is it enough to warrant the banning of drilling there?

   _____

   _____

   _____

   c. What does the University of Alaska, Fairbanks Institute of Arctic Biology report say concerning caribou distribution patterns and oil fields?

   _____

   _____

   _____

   _____

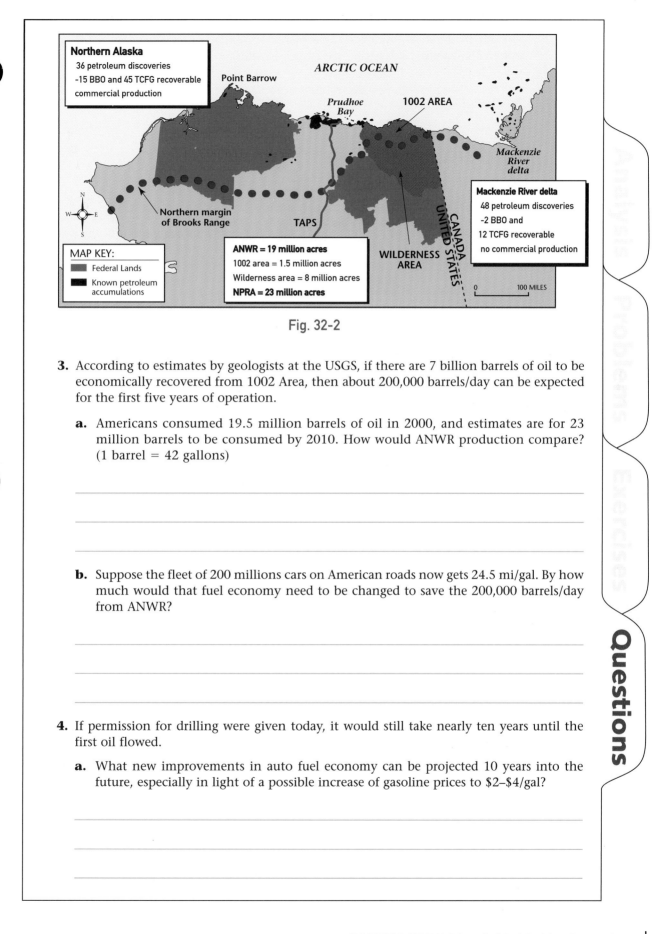

Fig. 32-2

3. According to estimates by geologists at the USGS, if there are 7 billion barrels of oil to be economically recovered from 1002 Area, then about 200,000 barrels/day can be expected for the first five years of operation.

   a. Americans consumed 19.5 million barrels of oil in 2000, and estimates are for 23 million barrels to be consumed by 2010. How would ANWR production compare? (1 barrel = 42 gallons)

   _____

   _____

   _____

   b. Suppose the fleet of 200 millions cars on American roads now gets 24.5 mi/gal. By how much would that fuel economy need to be changed to save the 200,000 barrels/day from ANWR?

   _____

   _____

   _____

4. If permission for drilling were given today, it would still take nearly ten years until the first oil flowed.

   a. What new improvements in auto fuel economy can be projected 10 years into the future, especially in light of a possible increase of gasoline prices to $2–$4/gal?

   _____

   _____

   _____

b. What are the implications about the future development of vehicles that use alternate fuels to gasoline: hybrids, fuel cells, hydrogen, etc?

_____

_____

_____

_____

_____

5. To protect the permafrost and surrounding tundra, drilling would only occur in the winter, when the average temperature is $-19°$ F and the ground can support the drilling equipment. Building, moving, and working large oil rigs in the Arctic requires large volumes of water.

a. What is the hydrology of the region?

_____

_____

_____

_____

_____

b. Is there enough water to satisfy industry and wildlife so that both can prosper?

_____

_____

_____

_____

_____

c. How does the transport of water in Arctic regions, in the dead of winter, contribute to the price of a barrel of oil and, therefore, to the amount that can be profitably recovered?

_____

_____

_____

_____

_____

_____

6. If global climate change is occurring, the *Laws of Thermodynamics* predict that the effects of temperature change will be more pronounced in the polar regions. With its unique ecosystem, could ANWR be a controlled experiment to monitor the effects of this projected climate change?

_____

_____

_____

_____

_____

_____

7a. What are ways to allow cost-effective industrial development in this environmentally fragile area with minimum impact on the local ecology?

_____

_____

_____

_____

b. What is the track record of the companies that are drilling now in the Prudhoe Bay area?

_____

_____

_____

_____

_____

_____

_____

_____

_____

_____

_____

Analysis   Problems   Exercises

Questions

Investigate the following Web sites to help get your research started. They all have search boxes. Type "drilling in ANWR" in the box for information.

CNN www.cnn.com

CNBC http://www.cnbc.com

United States Department of Energy http://www.energy.gov/

United States Fish and Wildlife Department on ANWR
          http://arctic.fws.gov/issues1.htm

Union of Concerned Scientists http://www.ucsusa.org/

USGS - ANWR, 1002 Area, Petroleum Assessment, Including Economic Analysis
          http://pubs.usgs.gov/fs/fs-0028-01/fs-0028-01.htm

American Petroleum Institute http://www.api.org/

The Sierra Club http://www.sierraclub.org/

The National Audubon Society http://www.audubon.org/

The Wilderness Society http://www.wilderness.org/

INVESTIGATION

33

Global Climate Change

PURPOSE

➤ Analyze and graphically depict interrelationships among a complex of effects of global warming

➤ Apply the analysis of effects to environmental, economic, and sociopolitical events, both locally and generally

INTRODUCTION

Research has shown that the surface temperature of Earth has risen about 1°F over the last one hundred years and the warming has been accelerating for the last 20 years, as shown in **Fig. 33-1**. The evidence is becoming overwhelming that humans are responsible for much of the warming over the last 50 years by adding large amounts of carbon dioxide, nitrous oxide, and methane to the atmosphere.

Fig. 33-1

The rise in temperature above the long-term mean appears to have accelerated since about 1980.

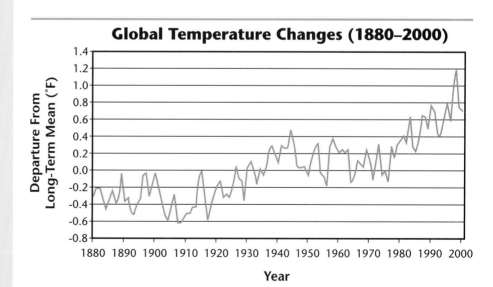

Global Temperature Changes (1880–2000)

For purposes of this investigation you will ignore the causes—and the blame—for global warming and concentrate on finding patterns in its comprehensive, large-scale effects. For example, increasing atmospheric temperature seems to be causing glaciers to recede, polar ice to thin and retreat, and plants to flower sooner in the spring. In addition, warm-climate southern plants and trees are migrating towards northern latitudes and up mountain slopes, the seasons are becoming more intensely hot and cold, some rainfall patterns may be changing, and there seems to be a bleaching of coral reefs. In this investigation you will connect and draw relationships among eleven other effects of global warming, using reliable sources to support your conclusions.

Materials

- print and Internet sources for researching effects of global warming

Procedure

Step 1 Write the name of each event below on a single post-it note.

- increased water runoff
- more frequent droughts and floods
- coastal flooding and damage
- reduced irrigation capacity
- overuse and pollution of water
- erosion and silting
- extreme weather
- acid rain
- sea level rise
- insect infestation
- changes in the water cycle (transpiration rate, soil moisture, rainfall patterns)

Step 2 Carry out research as needed to discover the causes and effects of the listed events.

Step 3 Refer to **Fig. 33-2.** Using the graphic organizer as a template, place the post-it notes in the ovals in such a way as to best illustrate the cause-and-effect relationships.

Global Climate Change

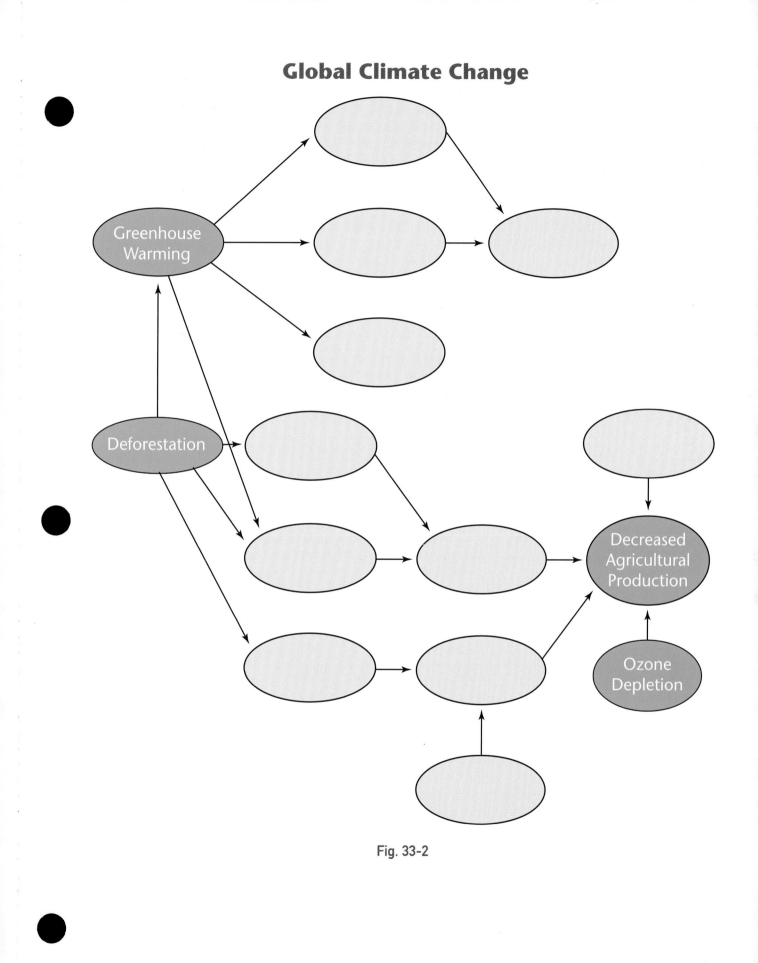

Fig. 33-2

1. Describe how two events in the organizer would directly impact your community.

   _____

   _____

   _____

   _____

2a. Follow one series of connections from the far left to the far right of the organizer. Describe in some detail how the cause on the left leads to the effect on the right.

   _____

   _____

   _____

   b. Outline two economic consequences of these events.

   _____

   _____

   c. Outline two social or political consequences of these events.

   _____

   _____

3a. Describe one food web in your region and how it would be impacted by the same changes you depicted in response to Question 2a.

   _____

   _____

   _____

   b. Explain specifically why some populations would increase and others would be harmed.

   _____

   _____

   _____

4. Develop an argument that predicts that agricultural land would be degraded by nutrient loss if carbon dioxide levels continue to climb at the present rate or faster.

   _____

   _____

   _____

Problems

Analysis

Exercises

Questions

Further Research *and* **Reading**

As you worked through this program, you found that there are a great variety of sources to learn about the environment and its workings. Your textbook and this lab manual are great places to start, but you should not limit yourself to just two sources of knowledge.

THE INTERNET

Each topic you study can be probed more deeply on the Internet. When you use the Internet as a source, be aware of where the information comes from; it is not always reliable. Most Web sites from college and university researchers are likely to be useful and of high quality. Also dependable are the sites from government agencies such as the EPA, United States Geologic Survey (USGS), National Oceanographic and Atmospheric Administration (NOAA), U.S. Department of Energy (DOE), NASA, U.S. Forest Service (USFS), U.S. Fish Game and Wildlife (USFGW), and others.

Some Web sites are mainly environmental in scope. One of the better ones is EurekAlert (www.eurekalert.org), maintained by the American Association for the Advancement of Science (AAAS). It is a general purpose science news Web site, but there are a lot of environmental topics that you can search.

The Environmental News Network (www.enn.com) is an excellent site that has four or more environmental news stories everyday. There are additional links for more in-depth reading. You can also sign up for an e-mail newsletter.

The EnviroLink Network (www.envirolink.org) Web site has about thirty subtopics that allow you to find information on topics from agriculture to wildlife. It also has four or five news articles from a variety of sources.

Environment and Energy Publishing LLC (www.eenews.net) has a Web site that is broken down into three sections. One, Environment and Energy Daily, deals with congressional legislation on energy-related issues. Another, Greenwire, tracks the politics, policies, and the press on energy issues. Lastly, Land Letter deals with natural resource policy.

JOURNALS AND PERIODICALS

Scientific journals are another excellent resource. Many have free access to their articles. Some require that you register as a user at no charge.

The premier science journal in the United States is *Science* (www.sciencemag.org). It is a weekly periodical that has news stories and frontier research articles that can be read by interested readers. An interesting section on the Web page is the Essays on Science and Society. These give perspective on the interaction of science, scientists, and society. Many are environmentally related.

Scientific American (www.sciam.com) is a monthly journal that has longer articles, some environmental in scope. There also are news and technology sections that are applicable.

The *New Scientist* (www.newscientist.com) is a British weekly that often has environmental topics highlighted. The articles also have suggested related stories to deepen your understanding of a topic.

The weekly *Science News* (www.sciencenews.org) does not post all its articles on its Web page, but it documents the references and sources so you can probe the topic.

Many newspapers have a weekly science section. An outstanding one is in the *New York Times*, where every Tuesday a whole section, (Science Times, www.nytimes.com/pages/science/index.html), is devoted to science. In recent years topics that have appeared there prior to the APES exam sometimes were the theme for a few free-response questions on the APES exam.

BOOKS

A major source of information and discovery is paperback books. These are inexpensive, often written for popular consumption, and not overly technical. Some large bookselling franchises, such as Barnes and Noble and Borders, have extensive science sections where you can find a variety of environmentally focused books. Many students who tried these books have said how surprised they were at how interesting a science book can be! No matter which ones you select, they will in some way be addressed during the year in this course. Some students find it stimulating to keep a diary of their comments, questions, and insights as they read. Below are some suggestions.

FURTHER READINGS IN ENVIRONMENTAL SCIENCE

Title	Author	Date
A CIVIL ACTION	Jonathan Harr	1996
A FIERCE GREEN FIRE	Philip Shabecoff	1993
A FINE PIECE OF WATER	Tom Anderson	2002
AGAINST THE TIDE—BATTLE FOR AMERICA'S BEACHES	Cornelia Dean	1999
A GREEN HISTORY OF THE WORLD	Clive Pointing	1992
ATMOSPHERE, CLIMATE AND CHANGE	Thomas Graedel and Paul Crutzen	1997
BECOMING HUMAN	Ian Tattersal	1998
BIOGEOCHEMISTRY OF A FOREST ECOSYSTEM	Gene Likens	1977
CADILLAC DESERT	Marc Reisner	1986
CHANGES IN THE LAND	William Cronon	1984
CLIMATE CHANGE: THE IPCC SCIENTIFIC ASSESSMENT	J. T. Houghton et al.	1990
DEEP ECOLOGY	Bill Devall	1985
DEGREES OF DISASTER: PRINCE WILLIAM SOUND	Jeff Wheelwright	1994
DESERT SOLITAIRE	Edward Abbey	1968

Title	Author	Date
DIGGING DINOSAURS	John Horner	1988
EARTH IN THE BALANCE	Al Gore	1992
EARTH UNDER SIEGE	Richard P. Turco	1997
ECOLOGY AND THE POLITICS OF SCARCITY	William Ophuls	1992
ECOLOGY, ECONOMICS, ETHICS: THE BROKEN CIRCLE	Bonnann and Kellert	1991
ECO-WARRIORS	Rick Scarce	1990
ENCOUNTERS WITH THE ARCHDRUID	John McPhee	1990
ENDURANCE: SHACKELTON'S LEGENDARY ANTARCTIC EXPEDITION	Caroline Alexander	1998
ENERGY: FROM NATURE TO MAN	Wiliam C. Reynolds	1974
EXTINCTION: BAD GENES OR BAD LUCK	David Raup	1992
FIELD GUIDE TO NATURE OBSERVATION AND TRACKING	Tom Brown	1983
FOUR CORNERS	Kenneth Brown	1995
GREEN DELUSIONS	Martin Lewis	1992
GUNS, GERMS AND STEEL	Jared Diamond	1999
HOW MANY PEOPLE CAN THE EARTH SUPPORT?	Joel E. Cohen	1995
INTO THE WILD	Jon Krakauer	1997
INTO THIN AIR: PERSONAL ACCOUNT OF THE MT. EVEREST DISASTER	Jon Krakauer	1998
ISAAC'S STORM	Eric Larson	1999
ISHMAEL	Daniel Quinn	1995
LAST REFUGE: ENVIRONMENTAL SHOWDOWN IN THE AMERICAN WEST	Jim Robbins	1994
LAST OASIS—FACING WATER SCARCITY	Sandra Postel	1992
LIFE IN THE BALANCE: HUMANITY AND THE BIODIVERSITY CRISIS	Niles Eldridge	2000
OF WOLVES AND MEN	Barry Lopez	1979
ON HUMAN NATURE	E. O. Wilson	1978
OUR COMMON FUTURE	World Commission on Environment and Development	1987
OUR ECOLOGICAL FOOTPRINT	Wackernagel and Rees	1996
PILGRIM AT TINKER CREEK	Annie Dillard	1974
PRISONER'S DILEMMA	William Poundstone	1993
REPLENISH THE EARTH	Lewis Regebstein	1991
RIVERS OF LIFE	Sandra Postel and Brian Richter	2003
SAND COUNTY ALMANAC	Aldo Leopold	1949
SILENT SPRING	Rachel Carson	1962
SOCIOBIOLOGY	E. O. Wilson	1975
SURELY YOU'RE JOKING, MR. FEYNMANN?	Richard Feynman	1985
TALES OF THE SHAMAN'S APPRENTICE	Mark Plotkins	1994
THE BURNING SEASON	Andrew Revkin	1990
THE COLD AND THE DARK: THE WORLD AFTER NUCLEAR WAR	Carl Sagan, Paul Ehrlich, et al.	1984
THE COMING PLAGUE	Laurie Garrett	1994
THE CONTROL OF NATURE	John McPhee	1990
THE COWBOY WAY	David McCumber	1999
THE DINOSAUR HERESIES	Robert Bakker	1986
THE DIVERSITY OF LIFE	E. O. Wilson	1999

Title	Author	Date
THE END OF NATURE	Bill McKibben	1990
THE LIMITS TO GROWTH, 2ND EDITION	Donella Meadows	1992
THE MONKEY WRENCH GANG	Edward Abbey	1975
THE NATURALIST	E. O. Wilson	1994
THE NIGHT OF THE GRIZZLIES	Jack Olsen	1969/96
THE PERFECT STORM	Sebastian Junger	1997
THE POPULATION BOMB	Paul Ehrlich	1997
THE POPULATION EXPLOSION	Paul and Anne Ehrlich	1990
THE SAND DOLLAR AND THE SLIDE RULE	Delta Willis	1996
THE SIXTH EXTINCTION	Richard Leakey	1996
THE SOLACE OF OPEN SPACES	Gretel Ehrlich	1985
THE SONG OF THE DODO	David Quammen	1997
THE STORK AND THE PLOW	Paul Ehrlich	1997
THE WARNING: THE ACCIDENT AT THREE MILE ISLAND	Mike Gray and Ira Rosen	1982
THREE SCIENTISTS AND THEIR GODS	Robert Wright	1988
TRACKING THE VANISHING FROGS	Kathryn Phillips	1994
WALDEN POND	Henry Thoreau	1854
WATERHEADS 3—10 CASES OF ENVIRONMENTAL ETHICS	Lisa Nelson and Catherine Dillingham	2002
WHY PEOPLE BELIEVE WEIRD THINGS	Michael Shermer	1998
WOLVES OF ISLE ROYALE	Rolk Peterson	1995

Also, always consider reading:

- Any geology or natural history title by John McPhee
- All books by Stephen J. Gould, Edward O. Wilson, Carl Sagan, and Edward Abbey

The goal of all these resources is to inspire you to be an interested, life-long learner on environmental issues. Most of the severe problems that face humans today in one way or another relate to the environment—problems involving over-population, energy production and fuels, potable drinking water supplies, natural resource depletion, global climate change, farms and food production, solid waste disposal, and toxic wastes. Even the economy and jobs are indirectly related to environmental issues. To be an effective citizen in this complex and modern world, it is important to understand environmental concerns and their ramifications.

Laboratory Investigations for AP Environmental Science